THE USBORNE
INTERNET-LINKED
PREHISTORIC WORLD

Fiona Chandler, Sam Taplin and Jane Bingham

Designed by Susie McCaffrey,
Steve Page and Susannah Owen

Consultants: Dr. David Norman and Dr. Anne Millard

Illustrated by Inklink Firenze,
Ian Jackson, Giacinto Gaudenzi, Gary Bines, David Wright,
Chris Shields, Peter Massey, Sean Milne and Andrew Robinson

Map illustrations by Jeremy Gower

Additional illustrations by Jeremy Gower, Bob Hersey,
Chris Lyon and Malcolm McGregor

Cover designer: Zoe Wray
Picture researcher: Sophy Tahta   Artwork co-o...
Managing editor: Jane Chisholm   Managing de...

D1472317

SCHOLASTIC INC.
New York Toronto London Auckland Sydney
Mexico City New Delhi Hong Kong Buenos Aires

Contents

Prehistoric Time

S cientists believe that the Earth was formed about 4,550 million years ago. This is such a vast length of time that it is almost impossible for anyone to imagine.

People have been around for only a tiny fraction of the time that the Earth has existed. If you think of all of prehistoric time as just one year, then the Earth would have been formed on January 1, but humans would not have appeared until one minute to midnight on December 31!

Experts divide prehistoric time into several periods, each lasting many millions of years. The diagram on these two pages shows the main prehistoric periods. You can also see when different plants and animals appeared on the Earth.

362 MILLION YEARS AGO

The first amphibians

408 MILLION YEARS AGO

DEVONIAN PERIOD (*say "div-ohn-ee-un"*)

440 MILLION YEARS AGO

SILURIAN PERIOD (*say "sy-loor-ee-un"*)

The first land plants

ORDOVICIAN PERIOD (*say "or-doh-vishy-un"*)

The first fish

The first creatures on land

510 MILLION YEARS AGO

CAMBRIAN PERIOD (*say "cam-bree-un"*)

The first creatures with skeletons

550 MILLION YEARS AGO

The first soft-bodied creatures

PRECAMBRIAN PERIOD (*say "pree-cam-bree-un"*)

The first living cells appear.

The Earth's surface is covered with volcanoes.

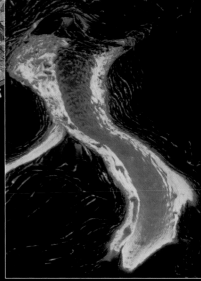

Hot, liquid rock pouring from a volcano

4,550 MILLION YEARS AGO
The Earth is formed.

The first
flying insects

CARBONIFEROUS PERIOD
(say "carbon-iffer-us")

290 MILLION YEARS AGO

The first
swimming
reptiles

PERMIAN PERIOD
(say "permy-un")

245 MILLION YEARS AGO

The first
dinosaurs

TRIASSIC PERIOD
(say "try-assick")

First forests

The first
reptiles

200 MILLION YEARS AGO

JURASSIC PERIOD
(say "jur-assick")

The first
mammals

The first birds

144 MILLION YEARS AGO

CRETACEOUS PERIOD
(say "cruh-tay-shuss")

The first
flowering plants

The first
humans

The first
horses

66 MILLION YEARS AGO

1.8 MILLION YEARS AGO

TERTIARY PERIOD
(say "ter-shuh-ree")

The first elephants

The first grasses

The first cats

QUATERNARY PERIOD
(say "kwot-en-uh-ree")

The end of
the dinosaurs

What Are Fossils?

Fossils are the remains of creatures and plants that lived millions of years ago. They provide a fascinating picture of life on Earth before any history was written down.

Fossils in the rock

Many fossils are made from animal bones or shells that have been preserved in rock. It takes millions of years for a fossil to form, but the process begins when a creature is buried under layers of sand and mud, called sediment. This usually happens under water, at the bottom of lakes, rivers or seas.

Gradually, the layers of sediment covering the creature are pressed down hard until they turn into rock. This layered rock is called sedimentary rock. Water trickles through the rock and soaks into the creature's skeleton. The water has minerals dissolved in it, which slowly harden (or crystallize), turning the skeleton into a fossil.

★
Fossil of an ammonite, a sea creature with a pearly shell

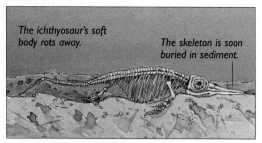

The ichthyosaur's soft body rots away.

The skeleton is soon buried in sediment.

A sea reptile, called an ichthyosaur, being buried in the seabed
★

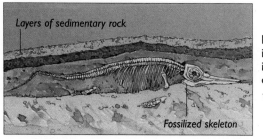

Layers of sedimentary rock

Fossilized skeleton

Fossil of an ichthyosaur inside layers of rock
★

Making shapes

Some skeletons that were buried in sediment have dissolved away, leaving their shapes in the rock. Some of the shapes have stayed empty, but others have been filled with hardened minerals, creating a fossil called a cast.

This shape was left by the skeleton of a starfish. ★

Coming to the surface

Fossils can now be found in sedimentary rocks on land, even though most fossils were originally formed under water. This is because, over millions of years, rocks that were once under water were gradually pushed up out of the water to become dry land (see page 15).

Buried bones

Experts have discovered many bones belonging to early humans and animals. Some of these bones were preserved in rock, but others were buried in very dry sand or in underground caves where no air could reach them.

The skull of an apelike ancestor of the first humans

Carbon fossils

Many plants and insects from prehistoric swamps were buried deep underground. Gradually, they heated up and turned into a sooty, black substance, called carbon. Most of the plants and creatures were squeezed together to make solid coal, but some formed delicate carbon fossils.

Soft-bodied survivors

It is very unusual to find fossils of creatures with soft bodies, but some have been discovered in the Burgess Shale, in Canada. These fossils were probably formed after a group of sea creatures were buried by a sudden mud slide. The mud then hardened into rock, creating very detailed fossils.

Fossil of a soft-bodied creature ★ called *Hallucigenia*

Trapped in amber

The bodies of some insects have survived for millions of years. These insects were stuck in sticky sap that oozed from trees. When the sap hardened, it turned into a yellow stone called amber, and any creatures trapped inside were perfectly preserved.

★
A prehistoric insect trapped in amber

Leaving traces

Some prehistoric creatures have left clear evidence of their way of life. Footprints made by animals and humans and trails made by creatures like worms have been preserved in hardened mud. Some eggs and droppings left behind by animals have also turned into fossils. All these kinds of evidence are known as trace fossils.

A dinosaur leaving its footprints in soft mud

Clues from Fossils

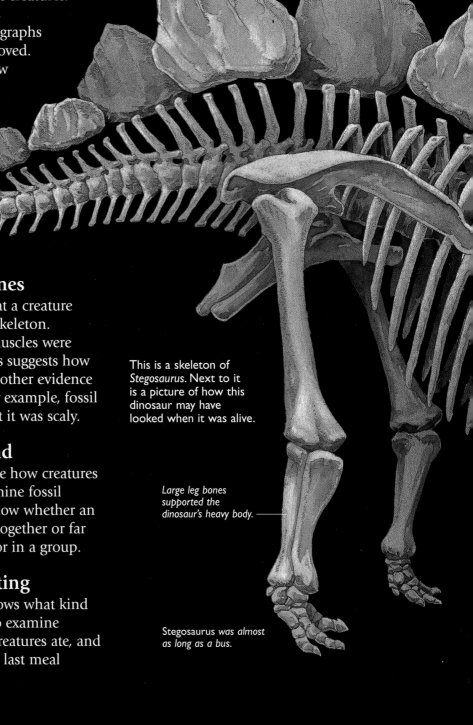

Experts who study fossils are called palaeontologists. By piecing together information from fossils, they can build up a surprisingly detailed picture of life on Earth millions of years ago.

Beginning with bones

Most fossils found by palaeontologists show the bones, teeth or shells of prehistoric creatures. When they discover a set of bones, palaeontologists take notes, photographs and sketches before anything is moved. This helps them to understand how the skeleton fits together.

Flesh on the bones

Experts can get a good idea of what a creature looked like from the shape of its skeleton. Markings on bones show where muscles were attached, and the size of the bones suggests how heavy an animal was. Sometimes, other evidence can help to build up a picture. For example, fossil prints of dinosaurs' skin show that it was scaly.

Moving around

As well as studying skeletons to see how creatures moved, palaeontologists also examine fossil footprints and trails. Footprints show whether an animal walked with its legs close together or far apart, and whether it lived alone or in a group.

Chewing and eating

The shape of an animal's teeth shows what kind of food it could chew. Experts also examine fossilized droppings to see what creatures ate, and occasionally they find an animal's last meal perfectly preserved in its stomach!

This is a skeleton of *Stegosaurus*. Next to it is a picture of how this dinosaur may have looked when it was alive.

Large leg bones supported the dinosaur's heavy body.

Stegosaurus *was almost as long as a bus.*

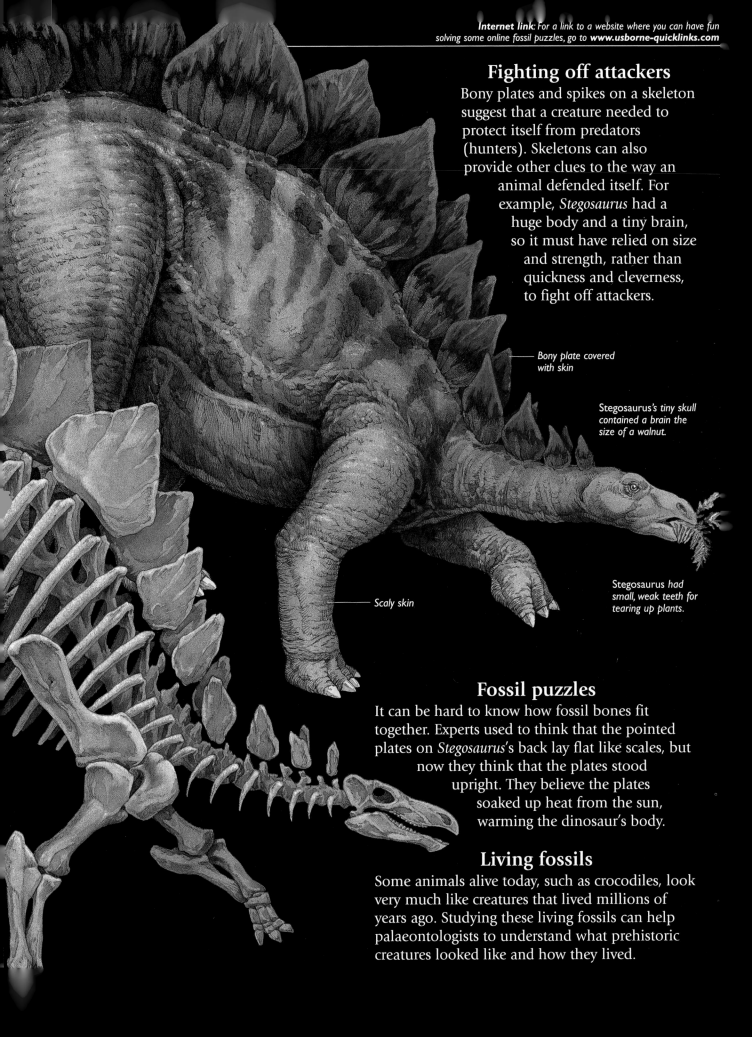

Fighting off attackers

Bony plates and spikes on a skeleton suggest that a creature needed to protect itself from predators (hunters). Skeletons can also provide other clues to the way an animal defended itself. For example, *Stegosaurus* had a huge body and a tiny brain, so it must have relied on size and strength, rather than quickness and cleverness, to fight off attackers.

Bony plate covered with skin

Stegosaurus's *tiny skull contained a brain the size of a walnut.*

Scaly skin

Stegosaurus *had small, weak teeth for tearing up plants.*

Fossil puzzles

It can be hard to know how fossil bones fit together. Experts used to think that the pointed plates on *Stegosaurus*'s back lay flat like scales, but now they think that the plates stood upright. They believe the plates soaked up heat from the sun, warming the dinosaur's body.

Living fossils

Some animals alive today, such as crocodiles, look very much like creatures that lived millions of years ago. Studying these living fossils can help palaeontologists to understand what prehistoric creatures looked like and how they lived.

The Story of Life

Many of the plants and animals that lived in prehistoric times were very different from those that are around today. This is partly because lots of prehistoric forms of life have died out, and partly because all living things gradually change with time.

The first creatures on Earth were very simple animals. Over millions of years, these creatures changed, or evolved, into new kinds of animals. This process of change is called evolution.

How evolution works

The first person to explain how evolution works was a scientist named Charles Darwin, who lived from 1809 to 1882. His general explanation is still accepted by scientists today.

Charles Darwin

Darwin realized that no two animals are exactly the same. For example, one deer may have slightly longer legs than another. Long legs are useful for escaping from attackers, so this deer will be more likely to survive and have young. The young may also have longer legs, like their parent. Over time, a new kind of longer-legged deer could evolve.

These pictures show how, with a series of small changes, one kind of animal can gradually evolve into a completely new creature.

★
4 Today's birds have hollow bones and no teeth, so their bodies are very light. Their strong wings are ideally suited for flying.

★
3 Feathered arms grew into wings. This early bird had teeth, like a dinosaur, and a heavy body.

★
2 Some two-legged dinosaurs grew feathers to keep themselves warm. Some also had beaks.

★
1 This is a typical two-legged dinosaur with scaly skin.

Fossil clues

The oldest fossils that have been found all show extremely simple forms of life. Fossils of complex creatures, such as reptiles and birds, are only found in much newer rocks. This suggests that living things did not appear on the Earth all at once, so they must have evolved gradually.

Animal families

To understand how one kind of animal could have evolved from another, scientists need to find out which animals are closely related. They do this by dividing them into groups.

All the members of a group have something in common with each other. The more things two animals have in common, the more closely they are related.

The biggest groups are called kingdoms. For example, all animals belong to the animal kingdom. Inside this group, there are smaller groups, with even smaller ones inside them.

The smallest group of all is known as a species. Animals that belong to the same species look very similar and can breed together.

Lions and leopards belong to different species, but both of them are big cats and members of the cat family.

Here you can see how big cats fit into different groups within the animal kingdom. As you read down the page, notice how the creatures in each new group have more and more in common with each other.

THE ANIMAL KINGDOM
(all animals)

VERTEBRATES
(all animals with a backbone)

MAMMALS
(all animals with hair that feed their young with milk)

CARNIVORES
(all meat-eating mammals)

THE CAT FAMILY

BIG CATS

Lions belong to a species called Panthera leo.

Leopards belong to a species called Panthera pardus.

Naming species

Scientists have given each species of plant and animal a special name. The name is written in Latin and is often a good description of the species. For example, the first humans that walked completely upright are known as *Homo erectus*, which means "upright man".

11

The Birth of the Earth

The Earth is a tiny planet in a vast universe. The universe is made up of billions of stars and planets and enormous clouds of gas, all separated by huge empty spaces. The stars are grouped in galaxies, each one containing millions of stars.

Our Sun is a small star in the Milky Way galaxy.

The Big Bang

Scientists think that the universe began over 15,000 million years ago with an unimaginably violent explosion, called the Big Bang. The Big Bang created a huge fireball, which cooled and formed tiny particles. Everything in the universe is made of these tiny particles, called matter.

These pictures show what may have happened after the Big Bang.

1 The fireball spread out and the universe began to expand. (It is still expanding today.)
★

2 As the fireball cooled, tiny particles collected into thick, swirling clouds of gas and dust.
★

3 The clouds pulled in more and more dust and gas. The gases became hotter until they began to burn, and stars formed.
★

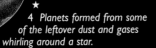
★

4 Planets formed from some of the leftover dust and gases whirling around a star.

Planet Earth

The Earth was formed about 4,550 million years ago from a cloud of dust and gas spinning around the Sun. Gradually, the Earth grew hotter and hotter, until it turned into a ball of liquid rock and metal. Lighter materials floated to the surface, where they cooled into a hard, rocky crust. The rocks underneath stayed hot and liquid.

This cutaway picture shows inside the Earth, as it is today.
★

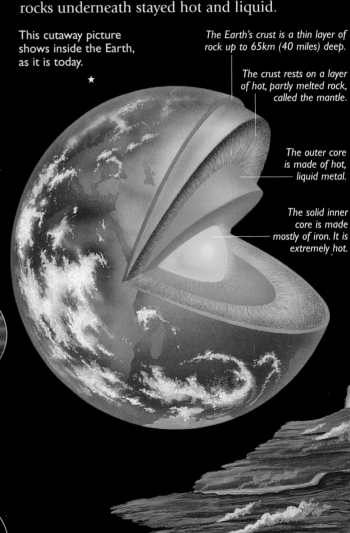

The Earth's crust is a thin layer of rock up to 65km (40 miles) deep.

The crust rests on a layer of hot, partly melted rock, called the mantle.

The outer core is made of hot, liquid metal.

The solid inner core is made mostly of iron. It is extremely hot.

A lifeless planet

For millions of years after the Earth was formed, nothing could live there. There was no water, no breathable air, and no protection from the harmful rays of the Sun. Volcanoes poured out red-hot liquid rock, and the Earth's surface was battered by giant rocks, called meteorites, that fell from space.

This scene shows how the Earth might have looked 4,000 million years ago.

There are no living creatures, because there is no oxygen for them to breathe.

Falling meteorites

The surface of the Earth is dry and rocky. There are no plants.

This huge hole, called a crater, was made by a meteorite smashing into the ground.

Liquid rock bubbles up through cracks in the Earth's crust.

The first oceans

Volcanoes on the Earth's surface sent out great clouds of steam and gas that collected in a thick layer around the Earth. As the clouds thickened and cooled, the steam turned into water, and it started to rain. It rained for thousands of years, flooding the Earth and creating the oceans.

Volcanoes pour out liquid rock from deep inside the Earth.

Liquid rock inside the Earth is called magma. When it reaches the surface, it is called lava.

The lava cools and hardens to form new rocks.

Volcanoes belch out clouds of gas and steam.

Boiling seas

Huge meteorites continued to batter the Earth until around 3,800 million years ago. As the meteorites hit the Earth's surface, they gave off heat. Scientists think that there may have been enough heat to make the oceans boil. This would have destroyed any very early forms of life.

THE EARTH

13

The Changing World

The Earth has not always looked the way it does today. Ever since our planet was formed, its surface has been changing. New rocks are being created all the time, and the land is constantly changing shape.

A giant jigsaw puzzle

The Earth's crust is divided into several huge pieces, called plates, which fit together like a gigantic jigsaw puzzle. Most plates are made up partly of dry land (known as continental crust) and partly of ocean floor (known as oceanic crust).

This picture shows some of the Earth's plates, with one of them lifted up.

Moving plates

The ground beneath your feet may seem solid, but it is actually moving. The plates that make up the crust are floating on hot, toffee-like rock just beneath the Earth's surface. This hot rock (or magma) moves around constantly, carrying the plates with it. Some plates are pushed together, while others are pulled apart.

This picture shows how the plates move around on the surface of the Earth.

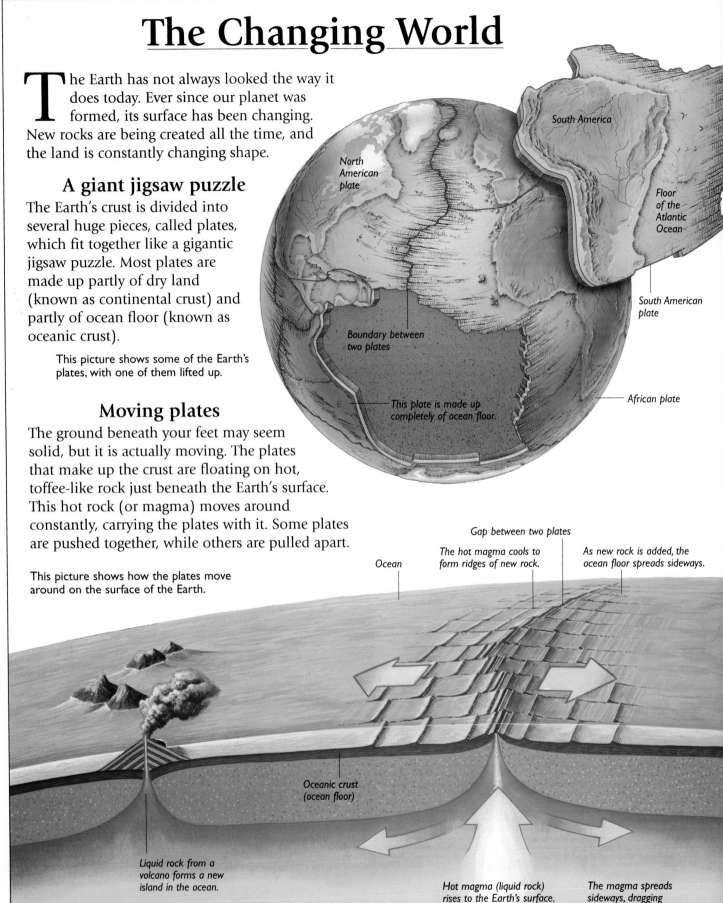

South America

North American plate

Floor of the Atlantic Ocean

South American plate

Boundary between two plates

This plate is made up completely of ocean floor.

African plate

Ocean

The hot magma cools to form ridges of new rock.

Gap between two plates

As new rock is added, the ocean floor spreads sideways.

Oceanic crust (ocean floor)

Liquid rock from a volcano forms a new island in the ocean.

Hot magma (liquid rock) rises to the Earth's surface.

The magma spreads sideways, dragging the plates apart.

Making mountains

This is Mount Everest, which is part of a group of mountains called the Himalayas. The Himalayas were formed when the plate carrying India crashed into the continent of Asia.

When two plates are pushed together, the land crumples up at the edges to form great ranges of mountains. Mountains formed like this are called fold mountains. They include some of the highest mountains in the world.

Drifting continents

The Earth's plates move at about the same speed that your fingernails grow. Over millions of years, this movement can make the continents drift huge distances. About 250 million years ago, all the continents joined to form a giant supercontinent called Pangaea, which then slowly split apart.

These maps show how Pangaea split up to form the continents we know today.

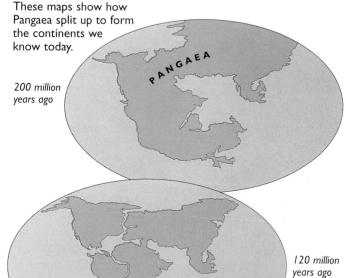

200 million years ago

120 million years ago

60 million years ago

Deep-sea trench

Volcano

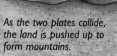

As the two plates collide, the land is pushed up to form mountains.

Continental crust (dry land)

Where two plates are pushed together, one is forced down under the other.

THE EARTH

15

The Beginning of Life

All living things are made up of tiny units, called cells. Cells are made mostly of chemicals called proteins, but where did these chemicals first come from?

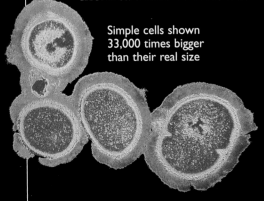

Simple cells shown 33,000 times bigger than their real size

Chemical soup

About 3,800 million years ago, the Earth's surface was covered in volcanoes which poured out poisonous gases. The gases dissolved in the warm water of the oceans, producing a kind of chemical "soup". Scientists think that these chemicals reacted with each other to form more complex chemicals, like the ones that make up proteins.

Electricity from lightning like this may have helped the chemicals to react.

From proteins to cells

Although scientists understand how the first proteins may have formed, they are not sure how these proteins came together to form something as complicated as a living cell.

The first cells may have formed in the seas. A film of proteins floating on the surface of the water may have broken up to form tiny spheres (balls) with chemicals trapped inside.

Cells could also have formed around hot water springs. The proteins may have melted together and then formed tiny, cell-like spheres as they cooled.

Another idea is that the clay at the bottom of shallow seas helped tiny blobs of protein to stick together and form some of the chemicals found in cells.

Blue bacteria

The first living things were made of just one cell each. They were rather like bacteria (germs). Millions of years later, some bacteria, known as blue-green algae, began to use sunlight and water to make their food. This process is called photosynthesis and it is how all plants live.

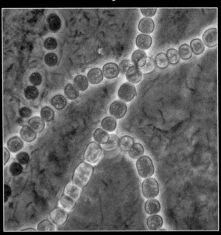

These blue-green algae have been magnified over 1,000 times.

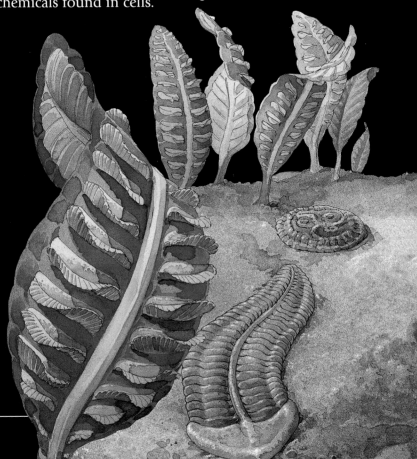

The first fossils

Stromatolites

The earliest evidence of life on Earth comes from fossils known as stromatolites, which contain the remains of large groups of blue-green algae. Some of them are 3,500 million years old.

Some algae in the early seas became trapped in a kind of chemical paste. The paste hardened into a glassy substance, preserving the algae as microscopic fossils.

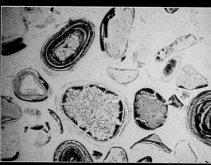

These fossilized algae were photographed under a powerful microscope.

A change of atmosphere

The Earth is surrounded by a thick layer of gases, called the atmosphere. For millions of years, the Earth's atmosphere contained no oxygen (the gas that animals need to breathe).

When plants make their food by photosynthesis, they produce oxygen. As the number of blue-green algae increased, oxygen began to build up in the atmosphere. This allowed many new forms of life to develop.

The first animals?

The earliest traces of animals are tracks left on the seabed by worms. The first animals had soft bodies, which do not fossilize easily, so it is very rare to find fossils of the animals themselves.

By 600 million years ago, a variety of weird and wonderful creatures had evolved. Some of them seem so strange that scientists are not sure if they are really animals at all.

The creatures in this scene lived in the sea from 600 to 550 million years ago.

The fossils of all these soft-bodied creatures were found in the Ediacara Hills of southern Australia.

Strange, disc-shaped creatures drift through the water.

These sea pens look like plants, but each one is actually a group of tiny animals.

This creature, called Spriggina, is a mystery. It may have been a type of flat, crawling worm.

Dickinsonia (a flat, worm-like animal) crawls over the seabed.

Creatures feed on the blue-green algae that covers the seabed.

Some scientists think Spriggina may have been attached to the sea floor by its "head".

Sea pens are attached to the seabed.

Tribrachidium, a mysterious jellyfish-shaped creature, creeps along the sea floor.

Shells and Skeletons

At first, life on Earth evolved very slowly. It took over 3,000 million years for simple cells to evolve into the first soft-bodied animals (see page 17). Then, around 550 million years ago, at the start of the Cambrian Period*, an amazing variety of new creatures began to appear in the seas.

Many of these new creatures had hard shells or outer skeletons to support and protect their soft bodies. Some of them also had legs with joints. Creatures with jointed legs and an outer skeleton are called arthropods.

A trilobite, a common Cambrian arthropod

The body is divided into segments.

Head

Each segment has a hard outer casing. This is the animal's skeleton.

Curious creatures

The fossils of some bizarre Cambrian creatures have been found in rocks known as the Burgess Shale, in Canada. These fossils are unusual because they show even soft-bodied creatures in fantastic detail. In some fossils, the animal's last meal can still be seen inside its body.

This scene shows some of the strange creatures of the Burgess Shale.

Sponges feed on tiny food particles which they suck in through holes in their bodies.

Marrella has long spines to protect itself from hunters.

Most sponges have spines to support and protect their soft bodies.

Wiwaxia's shimmering scales and sharp spines reflect the light and warn off hunters.

Marrella scuttles across the seabed, using its feelers to search for food.

Worms burrow in the seabed to avoid being eaten.

Ottoia is a fierce worm with rows of hooks and spines around its mouth.

Aysheaia has spiky feet for climbing around on the sponges that it eats.

A worm called Burgessochaeta uses its tentacles to feel for food.

The first hunters

At the start of the Cambrian Period, some animals began to hunt and eat other animals. Soft-bodied creatures may have grown shells and skeletons around this time, as a way of defending themselves.

EARLY LIFE

18   * Find out about prehistoric time periods on pages 4 and 5.

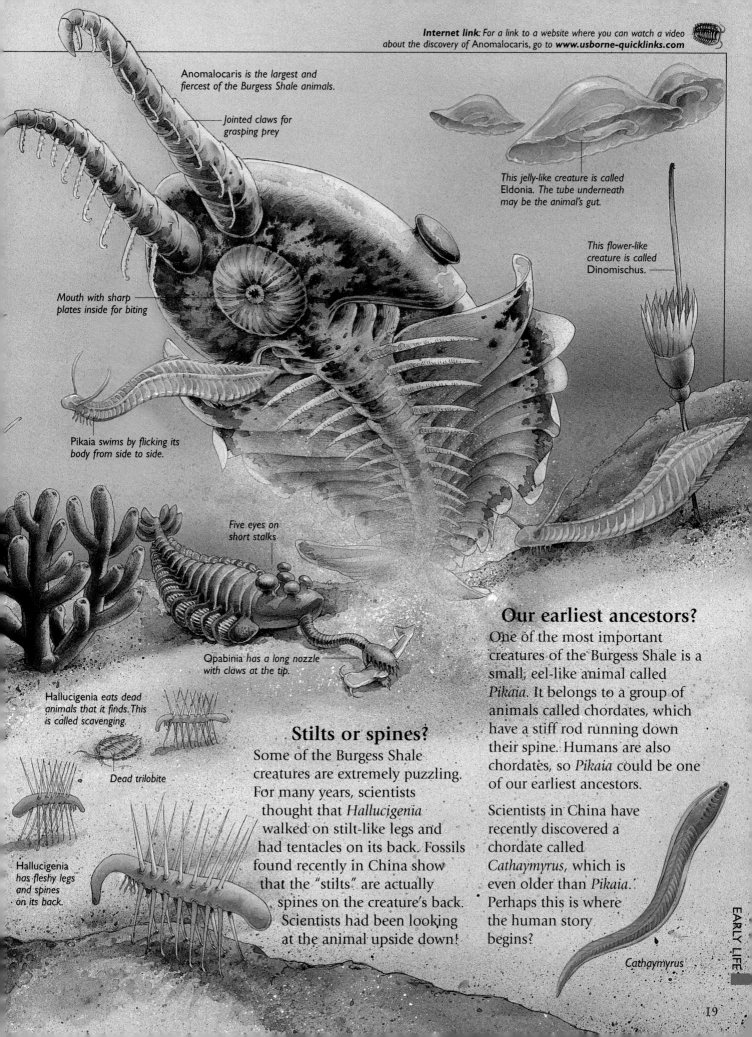

Anomalocaris *is the largest and fiercest of the Burgess Shale animals.*

Jointed claws for grasping prey

This jelly-like creature is called Eldonia. *The tube underneath may be the animal's gut.*

This flower-like creature is called Dinomischus.

Mouth with sharp plates inside for biting

Pikaia swims by flicking its body from side to side.

Five eyes on short stalks

Opabinia *has a long nozzle with claws at the tip.*

Hallucigenia *eats dead animals that it finds. This is called scavenging.*

Dead trilobite

Hallucigenia *has fleshy legs and spines on its back.*

Stilts or spines?

Some of the Burgess Shale creatures are extremely puzzling. For many years, scientists thought that *Hallucigenia* walked on stilt-like legs and had tentacles on its back. Fossils found recently in China show that the "stilts" are actually spines on the creature's back. Scientists had been looking at the animal upside down!

Our earliest ancestors?

One of the most important creatures of the Burgess Shale is a small, eel-like animal called *Pikaia*. It belongs to a group of animals called chordates, which have a stiff rod running down their spine. Humans are also chordates, so *Pikaia* could be one of our earliest ancestors.

Scientists in China have recently discovered a chordate called *Cathaymyrus*, which is even older than *Pikaia*. Perhaps this is where the human story begins?

Cathaymyrus

EARLY LIFE

19

The Crowded Seas

Around 510 million years ago, many of the strange Cambrian creatures died out. They were replaced by an enormous variety of new creatures which thrived in the warm, shallow seas of the Ordovician and Silurian Periods. Some of these creatures, such as starfish, sea lilies and corals, are still around today.

Colonies of corals

Corals are tiny, bag-like creatures that live together in large groups, or colonies. They use their tentacles to sweep food into their mouths.

Tentacle

Corals

Corals have hard, chalky skeletons that support their soft bodies. Over time, the skeletons build up to form rocky mounds called reefs. The first coral reefs appeared 450 million years ago, during the Ordovician Period.

Starfish on stalks

Starfish belong to a group of animals called echinoderms, which means "spiny-skinned". Their cousins, the sea lilies, are rather like starfish on stalks. Sea lilies have lots of waving arms covered in sticky suckers, which trap tiny particles of food.

Arms

The stalk is attached to the seabed.

Fossil of a prehistoric sea lily
★

This scene shows an Ordovician coral reef.

Bryozoans, or sea mats, form a lacy network of tiny tubes.

These corals live in a chain-shaped colony.

These corals live in a pie-shaped colony.

Trilobites hunt on the seabed.

Pieces of shell and skeleton from sea creatures help to build up a rocky reef.

Horn corals

Sea snails have teeth on their tongues for scraping food off the sea floor.

This is an early type of starfish.

Brachiopods, or lampshells, take in tiny food particles from the water.

Sea lilies, or
crinoids, wave
their arms in
the water to
catch food.

Sponge

Creatures in cups

Tiny creatures called graptolites also lived
in colonies. A colony of graptolites was
made up of lots of hard, horny cups all
linked together. Each cup contained a
single animal. Colonies may have lived
on the seabed or floated in the water.

A colony of graptolites

★

Each animal puts out
tentacles to catch food.

Horny cup

A nautiloid
hunts for food.

The shell has
hollow spaces
inside which help
the animal to float.

Tentacles covered
in suckers for
catching prey

Powerful predators

Animals that hunt and eat other animals are called
predators. During the Ordovician and Silurian
Periods, predators became experts at chasing and
catching their prey.

One group of predators were the nautiloids. They
had excellent eyesight and long, grasping tentacles
for catching food. Nautiloids were fast swimmers
and moved around by shooting water in and out
of their shells.

The most ferocious predators were the
eurypterids, or sea scorpions. The largest of
these was the giant *Pterygotus*, which grew
up to 2m (6ft 6in) long. It had sharp
pincers in front of its mouth, and used
its tail as a paddle for moving
quickly through the water.

Large eyes for
spotting prey

Paddle-shaped leg
for swimming
through the water

The sea scorpion has
caught a trilobite in
one of its pincers.

This is a giant sea scorpion
called Pterygotus.

The First Fish

Fish first appeared around 510 million years ago, at the beginning of the Ordovician Period. They were the first creatures that had a backbone to support their bodies. Animals with a backbone are called vertebrates.

Jawless fish

The first fish had no jaws for opening and closing their mouths. They lived at the bottom of the sea, where they could suck up small particles of food from the seabed.

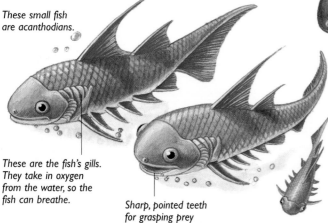

★ Sacabambaspis, an early jawless fish

— Hard, bony plating around the head and body

Fish with jaws

The first fish with jaws appeared during the Silurian Period. They are known as acanthodians, or "spiny sharks", although they were not actually sharks at all.

Fish that had jaws could use their mouths for grasping and biting, so they could eat a much greater variety of food. Many of them became hunters.

These small fish are acanthodians.

These are the fish's gills. They take in oxygen from the water, so the fish can breathe.

Sharp, pointed teeth for grasping prey

Ferocious fish

A group of fish called placoderms, or "plated skins", were particularly fierce hunters. Some placoderms were gigantic, and had powerful jaws lined with sharp, jagged plates of bone.

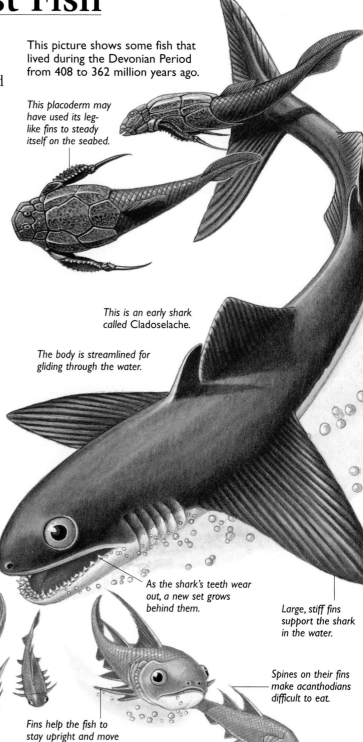

This picture shows some fish that lived during the Devonian Period from 408 to 362 million years ago.

This placoderm may have used its leg-like fins to steady itself on the seabed.

This is an early shark called Cladoselache.

The body is streamlined for gliding through the water.

As the shark's teeth wear out, a new set grows behind them.

Large, stiff fins support the shark in the water.

Spines on their fins make acanthodians difficult to eat.

Fins help the fish to stay upright and move quickly through the water.

The first sharks

Sharks first appeared during the Devonian Period. A shark's skeleton is not made of bone, but of cartilage (the same stuff that makes up the hard part of your nose). Cartilage is lighter than bone, and this helped the sharks to float.

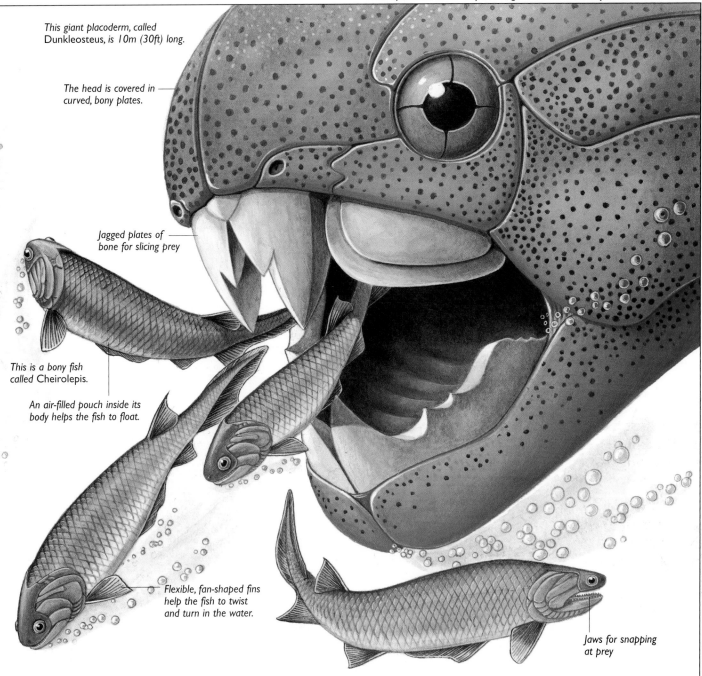

This giant placoderm, called Dunkleosteus, is 10m (30ft) long.

The head is covered in curved, bony plates.

Jagged plates of bone for slicing prey

This is a bony fish called Cheirolepis.

An air-filled pouch inside its body helps the fish to float.

Flexible, fan-shaped fins help the fish to twist and turn in the water.

Jaws for snapping at prey

Bony fish

Most fish that are alive today have bony skeletons. Almost all bony fish belong to a group known as "ray fins". They have delicate, fan-shaped fins supported by fine, bony rods (or rays).

A few bony fish belong to a group known as "fleshy fins". Their thick fins are mainly bone and muscle, with a fringe of fine rays around the edges. It was from these fish that the first land-living vertebrates evolved (see pages 26 and 27).

The coelacanth, a fleshy-finned fish which has hardly changed since Devonian times

EARLY LIFE

Life on Land

Life on Earth began in the seas. For millions of years, the Earth's surface was scorched by harmful ultraviolet light from the sun, and there was almost no life on land. Simple plants, called algae, grew at the edges of the sea, but the rest of the land was rocky and completely bare.

Gradually, a layer of gas called ozone built up around the Earth. The ozone blocked out some of the sun's rays and made it possible for plants and animals to survive on land.

Plants on land

The first known land plants appeared about 440 million years ago, near the end of the Ordovician Period. They were probably relatives of modern mosses and liverworts, and they only grew in very damp places.

Modern liverwort

Problems for plants

To survive on dry land, plants need roots to take in water from the ground and a network of tubes to carry the water from the roots to the stem. The outside of the plant has to be waterproof, so it doesn't dry out, and the stem must be strong enough to keep the plant upright.

The first known plant to have all these features was *Cooksonia*, which appeared about 420 million years ago.

★
Cooksonia

Animals on land

Once there were plants on land, there was food for animals to eat. The first creatures to move from water onto land were arthropods, such as spiders, millipedes and insects.

This picture shows some of the plants and animals that lived on land around 400 million years ago.

This leafless plant is called Aglaophyton.

Inside here are tiny cells, called spores, which blow away in the wind and grow into new plants.

Rhyniella *is a tiny, wingless insect.*

Centipedes have poisonous fangs for catching their prey.

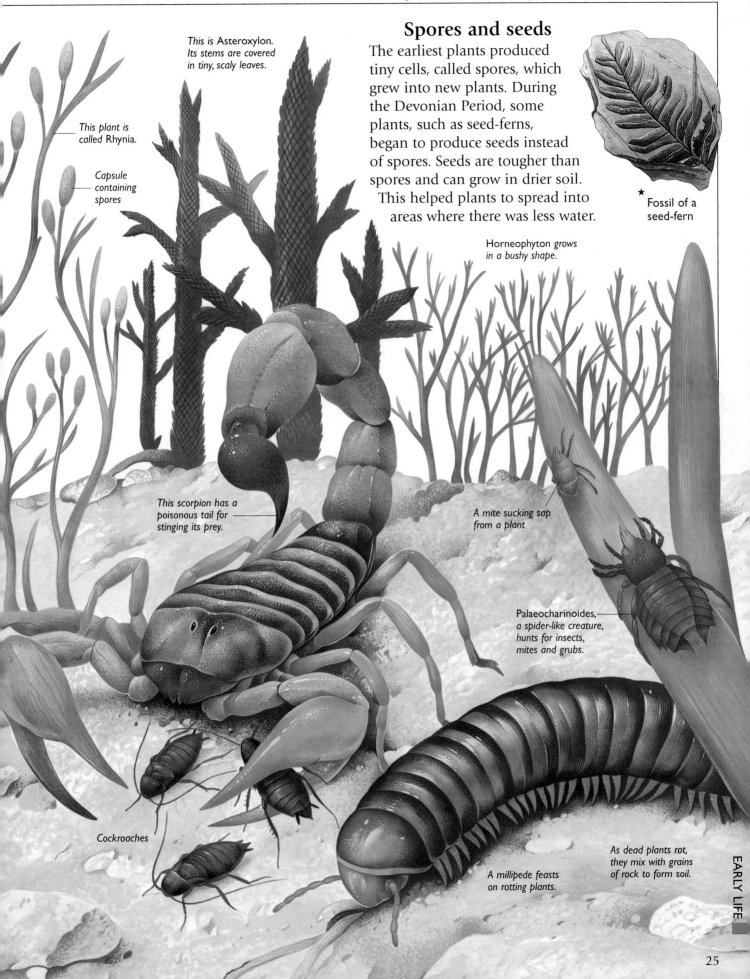

This is Asteroxylon. Its stems are covered in tiny, scaly leaves.

This plant is called Rhynia.

Capsule containing spores

Spores and seeds

The earliest plants produced tiny cells, called spores, which grew into new plants. During the Devonian Period, some plants, such as seed-ferns, began to produce seeds instead of spores. Seeds are tougher than spores and can grow in drier soil. This helped plants to spread into areas where there was less water.

★ Fossil of a seed-fern

Horneophyton grows in a bushy shape.

This scorpion has a poisonous tail for stinging its prey.

A mite sucking sap from a plant

Palaeocharinoides, a spider-like creature, hunts for insects, mites and grubs.

Cockroaches

A millipede feasts on rotting plants.

As dead plants rot, they mix with grains of rock to form soil.

EARLY LIFE

25

Fish out of Water

During the Devonian Period, the Earth's climate grew warmer, and there were long periods of dry weather. Lakes and rivers became shallower and contained less oxygen, so the fish that lived in them had to adapt in order to survive.

Lungs and legs

One group of fish, the "fleshy fins", had lungs as well as gills. This meant that they could breathe air if there wasn't enough oxygen in the water. They may have used their strong, muscular fins to push their heads above the water.

Why did fish grow legs?

Experts used to think that fish evolved legs so that they could walk to new ponds, if the pond where they were living dried up. Now, scientists believe that fish evolved legs and lungs to help them live in shallow water, rather than to help them get onto land.

A fleshy-finned fish called Eusthenopteron gulps air at the surface of the water.

Scientists believe that the muscular fins of these fish gradually evolved into four legs. The bones that supported their fins are very similar to the leg bones of land animals.

The fish uses its strong fins to prop itself up.

Fish with legs

One of the first four-legged animals was *Acanthostega*. It had gills for breathing under water and probably could not survive on land for long. With its short legs, it could move around in water even when the water was too shallow for swimming.

This fish, called Panderichthys, has four strong "arm" and "leg" fins, and no fins on its back.

Wide, fishy tail

Acanthostega uses its flipper-like legs for swimming.

Gills for breathing under water

Slim, streamlined body for gliding through the water

Onto the land

About 375 million years ago, an animal called *Ichthyostega* appeared. It lived mainly in the water, but it could also breathe air and crawl onto land. It probably returned to the water to lay its eggs. Animals that live on land, but lay their eggs in the water, are called amphibians.

This scene shows some creatures that would have lived in a shallow Devonian lake.

The back legs are too weak to be any use on land.

Ichthyostega drags itself around on its powerful front legs.

A strong ribcage supports the animal's lungs.

Fishy tail

In shallow water, Acanthostega pushes itself around on its short legs.

Each foot has eight toes for gripping the bottom of the lake.

Wide, paddle-like back leg

Big bones

Ichthyostega had a strong skeleton to support its large body. Animals that live only in water do not need a strong skeleton, because their bodies are supported by the water. Without a strong skeleton, the body of a land animal would collapse in on itself, crushing the soft parts inside.

In the water, Ichthyostega is a fast-moving hunter.

Gills

Powerful jaws for catching fish

EARLY LIFE

27

Swamps and Forests

At the start of the Carboniferous Period, 362 million years ago, large areas of the world were covered in swamps. The weather was warm and wet, and these vast, steamy swamps were ideal places for plants and trees to grow. Thick forests of gigantic trees spread out across whole continents.

The trees in a Carboniferous forest were very different from those that are around today. The tallest trees were the giant clubmosses (moss-like plants with upright stems). They had green, scaly bark and reached heights of 50m (150ft).

This scene shows some of the plants and creatures that lived in a Carboniferous coal swamp about 350 million years ago.

Lepidodendron *is the tallest of the giant clubmosses.*

Meganeura, *a giant dragonfly, has wings that measure 60cm (2ft) across.*

A giant millipede feeds on rotting leaves.

A microsaur, a lizard-like amphibian, lounges on a fallen tree trunk.

Keraterpeton *uses its long tail for swimming.*

Diplocaulus *has strange fins on its head to help it swim.*

Gephyrostegus *has spiky teeth for eating insects.*

Creating coal

Dead plants and fallen trees piled up on the forest floor, and were gradually buried under layers of mud. Over millions of years, the plants and trees were squeezed until they hardened and turned into coal. This coal is still being mined in some parts of the world today.

Big bugs

The Carboniferous swamps swarmed with huge insects, spiders and bugs. Giant dragonflies, the first creatures with wings, fluttered through the trees. Millipedes up to 2m (6ft 6in) long crept around in the dead leaves, and enormous spiders spun simple webs to catch their prey.

The age of amphibians

During the Carboniferous Period, a great variety of amphibians evolved. Some were small, lizard-like creatures that scampered around on the forest floor in search of insects to eat. Some hunted in the water like crocodiles. Others gradually lost their legs and could no longer live on land at all.

Like amphibians today, the early amphibians laid their soft, jelly-covered eggs in ponds or streams. This meant that they had to stay close to water. If animals were going to live successfully on land, they had to find a way around this problem.

This clubmoss, called Sigillaria, has no branches, just a clump of leaves.

Giant horsetail

Tree-fern

Short ferns and horsetails grow at ground level.

A spider waits for insects to fly into its web.

Pholidogaster, a large, crocodile-like creature, hunts fish and smaller amphibians.

This lizard-like animal, known as "Lizzie", may have spent all of its life on dry land.

Ophiderpeton is a legless, eel-like amphibian.

EARLY LIFE

29

What Are Reptiles?

Around 300 million years ago, a new group of creatures, called reptiles, evolved from amphibians. Reptiles were the first vertebrates (animals with a backbone) that were able to live on land all the time. Present-day reptiles, such as lizards, crocodiles and tortoises, show us how the early reptiles may have lived.

Keeping warm

Reptiles are ectothermic, or cold-blooded. This means that they cannot produce their own heat. Instead, they rely on heat from the sun to keep their bodies warm.

A crocodile warming itself in the sun

At night, reptiles get cold and have to rest. In the morning, they lie in the sun until their bodies warm up. Then, they can start to move around in search of food.

Land legs

Animals that live on land need strong legs to lift their bodies off the ground, so they can move around easily. A typical reptile has legs that stick out on either side of its body. As the animal runs, its whole body twists from side to side, so its skeleton needs to be very strong and flexible.

Scaly skin

On land, animals lose water all the time through their skin. If they lose too much water, they dry up and die. Reptiles have scaly, waterproof skin to stop their bodies from drying out.

This picture shows *Hylonomus*, one of the earliest known reptiles.

Hylonomus is about 20cm (8in) long.

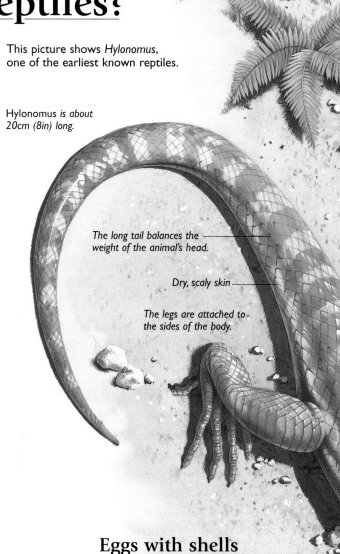

The long tail balances the weight of the animal's head.

Dry, scaly skin

The legs are attached to the sides of the body.

Eggs with shells

Reptiles lay their eggs on dry land, instead of in the water as amphibians do. Reptile eggs have a leathery, waterproof shell which protects the baby inside and stops it from drying out. The baby grows inside the egg and only hatches out when it is big enough to survive on its own.

★ Inside a reptile egg

The yolk provides food for the baby reptile.

Baby reptile

A bag of liquid protects the baby from knocks.

Shell

Recognizing reptiles

Scientists identify early reptiles by the shape of their skulls and jaws. The first reptiles had a more powerful bite than their amphibian ancestors. This made them better hunters and also allowed them to eat plants for the first time.

The first reptiles

The earliest known reptiles, such as *Hylonomus*, were small, lizard-like creatures. They were well suited to life on land and did not need to live close to water. This meant that they could spread out into drier areas. These small creatures were the ancestors of every type of land animal alive today.

Hylonomus eats insects, such as these cockroaches.

Sharp, pointed teeth for cracking open the bodies of insects

The reptile twists its body from side to side as it runs.

Hylonomus has strong ribs and lungs to pump air in and out of its body.

Long toes for gripping the ground

Early Reptiles

Once reptiles had evolved, they spread out very quickly on land. By 290 million years ago, at the start of the Permian Period, several new types of reptiles had appeared. Some of these new reptiles were large meat-eaters, or carnivores, that hunted other reptiles. Others were plant-eaters, or herbivores.

Early plant-eaters

A pareiasaur, an early plant-eating reptile

One group of small, plant-eating reptiles had chisel-shaped teeth which they may have used for digging up roots. Other plant-eaters, called pareiasaurs, were as big as a hippo. Pareiasaurs had strong, blunt teeth for grinding up plants. Their backs and heads were covered in hard, bony plates.

Sails of skin

During the Permian Period, the largest and most successful animals were a group of reptiles known as synapsids. Some early synapsids had a tall sail of skin on their backs, which they probably used to control their body temperature.

This picture shows some sail-backed synapsids.

The sail soaks up heat from the sun, warming the reptile's body.

Bony spine

The reptiles cool down by turning their bodies around, so the thin edge of the sail faces the sun.

Edaphosaurus *is a plant-eater. Its jaws are lined with blunt, chisel-shaped teeth.*

Dimetrodon *is a meat-eater. It has two types of teeth for stabbing and slashing its prey.*

When the reptile walks, its long body twists from side to side.

REPTILES

Longer legs

About 270 million years ago, the synapsid reptiles began to change. Instead of having short, sprawling legs, they developed longer legs that grew directly under their bodies. This allowed them to take bigger strides and move around faster. These new, improved reptiles are known as therapsids.

This scene shows *Moschops*, a plant-eating therapsid, being attacked by a group of smaller meat-eaters, called *Lycaenops*.

Moschops is 5m (16ft) long and has a huge, barrel-shaped body.

Back to the water

Although reptiles had evolved to cope with life on dry land, some reptiles went back to living in the water. One of the earliest to do this was *Mesosaurus*.

Mesosaurus, an early sea reptile ★

Mesosaurus had long, spiky teeth which it used to trap small, shrimp-like creatures in its mouth. It may have had a fin on its tail and webbed feet to help it swim.

Land and sea

During the Permian Period, all the Earth's continents joined together to form one giant supercontinent (see page 15). This meant that reptiles could spread out to all parts of the world. At the same time, vast numbers of sea creatures died out, because the shallow seas around the continents disappeared.

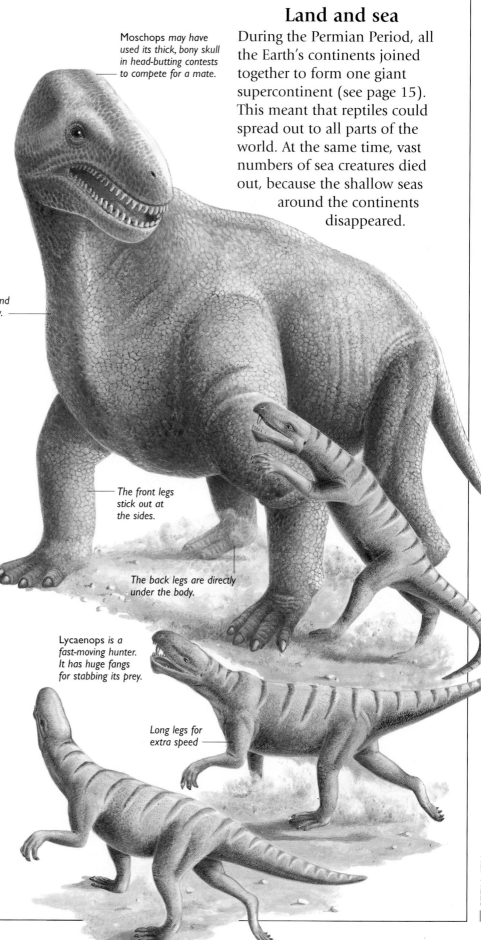

Moschops may have used its thick, bony skull in head-butting contests to compete for a mate.

The front legs stick out at the sides.

The back legs are directly under the body.

Lycaenops is a fast-moving hunter. It has huge fangs for stabbing its prey.

Long legs for extra speed

REPTILES

33

The Rise of the Reptiles

At the start of the Triassic Period, about 245 million years ago, the most common creatures on Earth were animals known as cynodonts (say "sigh-no-donts") and dicynodonts (say "die-sigh-no-donts"). These were both new types of therapsid reptiles (see page 33).

Tusks and beaks

Dicynodonts were plant-eaters. They had two tusks at the sides of their jaws for digging up roots, and a tough beak for slicing through plant stems. They ground up their food using sharp, horny plates on the roof of their mouths.

Reptiles with fur

Cynodonts had slim, dog-like bodies and long legs. They also had powerful jaws lined with different types of teeth for cutting, stabbing and chewing. Some cynodonts probably grew fur to help keep their bodies warm. Unlike other reptiles, they may even have been able to produce their own body heat.

Near the end of the Triassic Period, furry cynodonts evolved into a completely new group of animals, called mammals (see pages 52 and 53).

This scene shows some cynodonts and dicynodonts.

Lystrosaurus, a typical dicynodont, pulls up plants with its tusks.

Tough, horny beak

Lystrosaurus has a barrel-shaped body and short, stout legs.

Whiskers

Long, slim body

A cynodont called Thrinaxodon with its pups

Fur helps to keep heat inside the body.

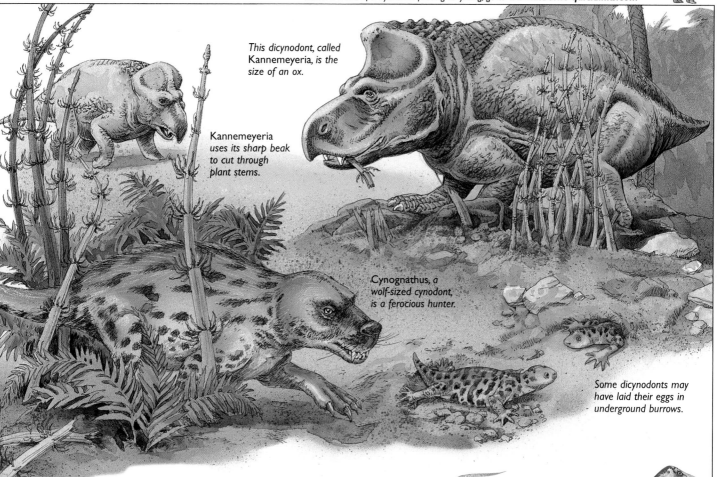

This dicynodont, called Kannemeyeria, is the size of an ox.

Kannemeyeria uses its sharp beak to cut through plant stems.

Cynognathus, a wolf-sized cynodont, is a ferocious hunter.

Some dicynodonts may have laid their eggs in underground burrows.

Ruling reptiles

Another group of reptiles that lived in the Triassic Period were the archosaurs, or "ruling reptiles". Early archosaurs had rows of bony plates along their backs. While they were resting, their legs sprawled out to the sides. However, they could also tuck their legs under their bodies to help them run faster.

Later in the Triassic Period, some archosaurs began to walk on their back legs, rather than on all fours. They had a short body and a long tail to help them keep their balance.

★ Lagosuchus, a two-legged archosaur, was a fast runner.

★ Eoraptor, one of the first dinosaurs, was a fast-moving hunter.

★ Euparkeria, an early archosaur, ran on all fours.

★ Stagonolepis was a crocodile-like archosaur with bony plates on its back.

The first dinosaurs

About 225 million years ago, the first dinosaurs evolved from small, two-legged archosaurs, such as *Lagosuchus*. Dinosaurs were different from other reptiles because they had longer, more upright legs that swung from front to back, instead of sticking out at the sides.

Once dinosaurs had evolved, many new types appeared. Their upright legs could carry a lot of weight and helped them to run fast. For the next 160 million years, they were the largest, strongest and fastest land animals in the world.

Meat-eating Monsters

The first dinosaurs on Earth were meat-eaters. Meat-eating dinosaurs are known as theropods, which means "beast foot". All theropods walked on their two back legs and had viciously sharp claws on their feet.

The earliest theropods were fairly small, less than 1.5m (5ft) from nose to tail. They had long, powerful legs for running fast and used their clawed hands for grasping prey.

A wide variety of theropods evolved from these early dinosaurs. Many of them stayed small and agile, but others grew monstrously large.

Beaks and brains

One group of theropods, known as "ostrich dinosaurs", had beaks instead of teeth. They had larger brains than most reptiles and were probably fairly intelligent.

Gallimimus, an ostrich-like theropod ★

Ostrich dinosaurs were very fast runners, and may have reached speeds of over 55km (35 miles) an hour.

Small and speedy

One of the smallest dinosaurs was *Compsognathus*, which was no bigger than a cat. It hunted lizards and other tiny animals, and used its long tail to help it balance as it ran.

Compsognathus ★ chasing a lizard

Clawed hands for holding onto prey

★ *Coelophysis*

Fast and fierce

Coelophysis was a ferocious and fast-moving hunter. It had a slim body with hollow bones, which made it very light and agile. It used its sharp, saw-like teeth to slice up its prey, and may even have eaten its own young.

Oviraptor ★

Killer claws

Deinonychus was only about 2m (6ft 6in) long, but it was a fierce hunter. It leaped on its prey and held on with its hands. At the same time, it kicked with the huge claws on its back feet. *Deinonychus* may have hunted in groups to tackle larger prey.

Egg snatchers

Some theropods may have fed on eggs that they stole from the nests of other dinosaurs. *Oviraptor* had a strong, stumpy beak with sharp edges for cracking open thick-shelled eggs.

Tyrannosaurus is taller than a modern giraffe.

The dinosaur's huge head is 1.3m (4ft) long.

Deinonychus

Curved teeth with sharp, saw-like edges for ripping flesh

Tyrannosaurus may have used its tiny arms to push itself up after resting.

Huge hunters

The largest theropods belonged to a group known as carnosaurs. They had massive heads, strong necks, powerful legs and short arms. One of the biggest carnosaurs was *Tyrannosaurus rex*, which was 14m (46ft) long. As well as hunting for food, it may also have eaten dead animals that it found.

Tyrannosaurus is too heavy to run long distances. It lies in wait and then charges full-speed at its prey.

★ *Tyrannosaurus rex charging at its prey*

REPTILES

37

Gentle Giants

The biggest land animals that ever lived were a group of dinosaurs called sauropods. They were plant-eaters with large bodies, small heads, and extremely long necks and tails.

Early sauropods

The early sauropods were much smaller than their later relatives, measuring only 4-6m (13-20ft) from nose to tail. Unlike meat-eating dinosaurs, they walked mainly on all fours. However, some early sauropods could stand up on their back legs to eat leaves from trees.

An early sauropod

Huge and heavy

The really gigantic sauropods appeared about 160 million years ago, during the Jurassic Period. An animal named *Seismosaurus* is thought to have been the biggest. It was probably 40-50m (130-165ft) long and may have weighed as much as 20 African elephants!

This scene shows some giant sauropods from the Jurassic Period.

Sauropods usually walk on all fours.

Diplodocus has a strong, arched back to carry the weight of its massive stomach.

The long neck is balanced by the weight of the tail.

Tiny head

Whip-like tail for lashing out at attackers

Strong, pillar-like legs

Diplodocus is longer than two buses placed end to end.

Like all sauropods, Seismosaurus spends most of its time feeding.

Weight lifting

Sauropods needed massive leg bones to support their great weight. Their backbones were also very strong, but they were sometimes cut away at the sides, instead of being solid. This made the animals lighter, so they had less weight to carry.

Hard to swallow

Sauropods had gappy, peg-like teeth which only grew at the front of their mouths. Teeth like this were ideal for stripping the leaves off trees, but were hopeless for chewing, so sauropods had to swallow their food whole.

Stomach stones

Plants and leaves are tough and very hard to digest, especially if they haven't been chewed properly. To help break down their food, sauropods swallowed large pebbles. These stones tumbled around in the animal's huge stomach, grinding the plants into a thick soup.

On its back legs, Apatosaurus can reach leaves high up in the trees.

Some sauropods have nostrils on top of their heads.

The dinosaur props itself up with its tail.

A group of sauropods can completely wreck a forest.

★
Brachiosaurus has long front legs, so it doesn't need to stand up on its back legs to reach the treetops.

Big bodyguards

Sauropods lived in large groups, or herds. When the herd was on the move, the larger adults walked on the outside of the group, with the baby dinosaurs in the middle. This made it harder for predators (hunters) to attack the babies.

REPTILES

39

Beaks and Crests

Some plant-eating dinosaurs, called ornithopods, were fast-moving and agile. They had bird-like feet and a horny beak for nipping off leaves and shoots to eat. All ornithopods could run on their two back legs to escape from predators (hunters).

Biting and chewing

One early ornithopod, called *Heterodontosaurus*, had large tusks behind its beak. It may have used these to defend itself against predators or rival males. *Heterodontosaurus* was one of the first dinosaurs to have cheeks. These stopped any food from falling out of the animal's mouth while it was chewing.

Heterodontosaurus
★

Small and swift

A small ornithopod called *Hypsilophodon* was a particularly fast runner, probably reaching speeds of 45km (30 miles) an hour. It had long legs and used its stiff tail to help it balance while running.

★
Hypsilophodon

Spikes and hoofs

Iguanodon was a large, heavy ornithopod, measuring up to 10m (33ft) long. It had a vicious spike on each thumb, which it used to fight off attackers. Its three middle fingers had hoofs, so it must have walked on all fours some of the time.

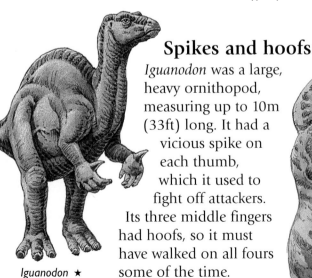
Iguanodon ★

Duck-billed dinosaurs

By about 80 million years ago, the most common plant-eating dinosaurs on Earth were a group of ornithopods known as hadrosaurs, or duck-billed dinosaurs. They had broad beaks, powerful jaws and thousands of small, sharp teeth for grinding up tough plants.

Broad, horny beak for slicing through plants

★ Adult hadrosaurs feed on pine needles and flowering plants, such as magnolia.

Incredible crests

Many hadrosaurs had strange spikes or crests on their heads. Some of these crests had hollow tubes inside. By blowing air through its crest, a hadrosaur may have been able to make booming noises to warn others of danger, or to attract a mate.

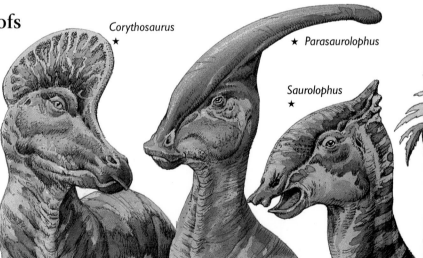
Corythosaurus
★

★ *Parasaurolophus*

Saurolophus
★

Mothers and babies

Hadrosaurs lived together in large herds. At the same time each year, the herd returned to the same place, so the females could lay their eggs. Unlike most reptiles, hadrosaurs guarded their eggs carefully, and looked after their babies until they could survive on their own.

This picture shows a group of hadrosaurs with their babies.

This hadrosaur is building a nest to lay her eggs in.

The nest is made of sand scraped into a mound.

The middle of the nest is hollowed out and filled with leaves.

This hadrosaur is guarding her eggs.

Each nest measures about 3m (10ft) across and contains up to 20 eggs.

This hadrosaur has brought back some berries for her babies to eat.

This baby is just hatching out. It is only 35cm (14in) long.

The babies stay in the nest while their mother goes to find food for them.

Horns, Clubs and Spikes

Some plant-eating dinosaurs were too big and heavy to escape from the fierce, meat-eating dinosaurs that hunted them. Instead, they developed a range of horns, clubs and spikes to protect themselves from predators.

Spikes and clubs

Ankylosaurs were covered from head to tail with bony plates. Vicious-looking spikes grew from these plates, and some ankylosaurs had a bony lump at the end of their tails, which they swung around like a club.

Bone heads

The pachycephalosaurs, or bone-headed dinosaurs, had a thick dome of solid bone on the top of their heads. They charged headfirst at their opponents, using their enormous skulls as battering rams.

Two bone-headed dinosaurs charging at each other
★

Head-banging contests

As well as fighting off hunters, bone-headed dinosaur males probably fought each other to prove which was the strongest. They may have banged their skulls together until the weakest gave up.

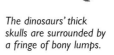

The dinosaurs' thick skulls are surrounded by a fringe of bony lumps.

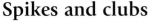

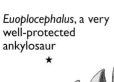

Euoplocephalus, a very well-protected ankylosaur
★

Euoplocephalus can swing its tail with great force.

Plates, knobs and spikes protect this dinosaur.

Pointed plates

Stegosaurs had two rows of upright plates running along their backs. The plates protected the stegosaurs from attack. They were probably also used to soak up heat from the sun, like the sails of the sail-backed reptiles (see page 32).

Bony plates covered with skin

Stegosaurus, the ★ largest known stegosaur

Internet link: For a website with a fact file about Stegosaurus, go to **www.usborne-quicklinks.com**

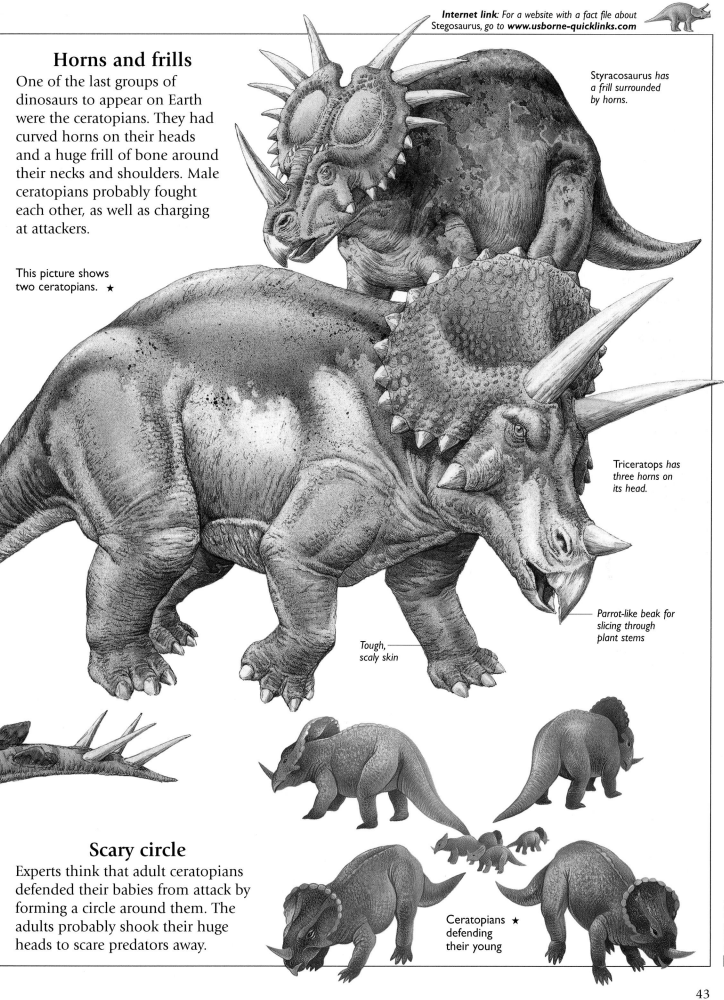

Horns and frills

One of the last groups of dinosaurs to appear on Earth were the ceratopians. They had curved horns on their heads and a huge frill of bone around their necks and shoulders. Male ceratopians probably fought each other, as well as charging at attackers.

This picture shows two ceratopians. ★

Styracosaurus has a frill surrounded by horns.

Triceratops has three horns on its head.

Parrot-like beak for slicing through plant stems

Tough, scaly skin

Scary circle

Experts think that adult ceratopians defended their babies from attack by forming a circle around them. The adults probably shook their huge heads to scare predators away.

Ceratopians ★ defending their young

Reptiles of the Seas

While the dinosaurs were living on the land, other reptiles were swimming in the seas. Reptiles probably entered the oceans about 290 million years ago (see page 33). Gradually, their bodies changed to help them live under water.

Early sea reptiles

By the start of the Triassic Period, about 245 million years ago, there were two kinds of reptiles living in the sea. Placodonts were turtle-shaped creatures. Some of them were good swimmers, but others spent most of their time on dry land.

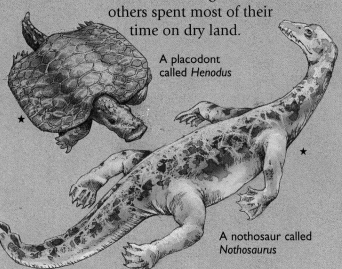

A placodont called *Henodus*

A nothosaur called *Nothosaurus*

Nothosaurs had long, thin bodies that could glide smoothly through the water, and they may have had webbed feet as well. They used their big, sharp teeth for catching fish.

Swimming with flippers

At the start of the Jurassic Period, around 200 million years ago, a group of long-necked reptiles called plesiosaurs evolved. Instead of legs, plesiosaurs had big, paddle-shaped flippers which they flapped like wings as they moved through the water.

Sea monsters

Some plesiosaurs became ferocious hunters. One group, called the pliosaurs, had massive jaws full of sharp teeth for stabbing their prey. Pliosaurs hunted in the depths of the oceans, searching for sharks, big squids and other swimming reptiles. Some pliosaurs were enormous, reaching lengths of over 12m (40ft).

This picture shows some reptiles that lived in the Jurassic seas.

Peloneustes is a fast-moving pliosaur.

This squid-like creature is called a belemnite.

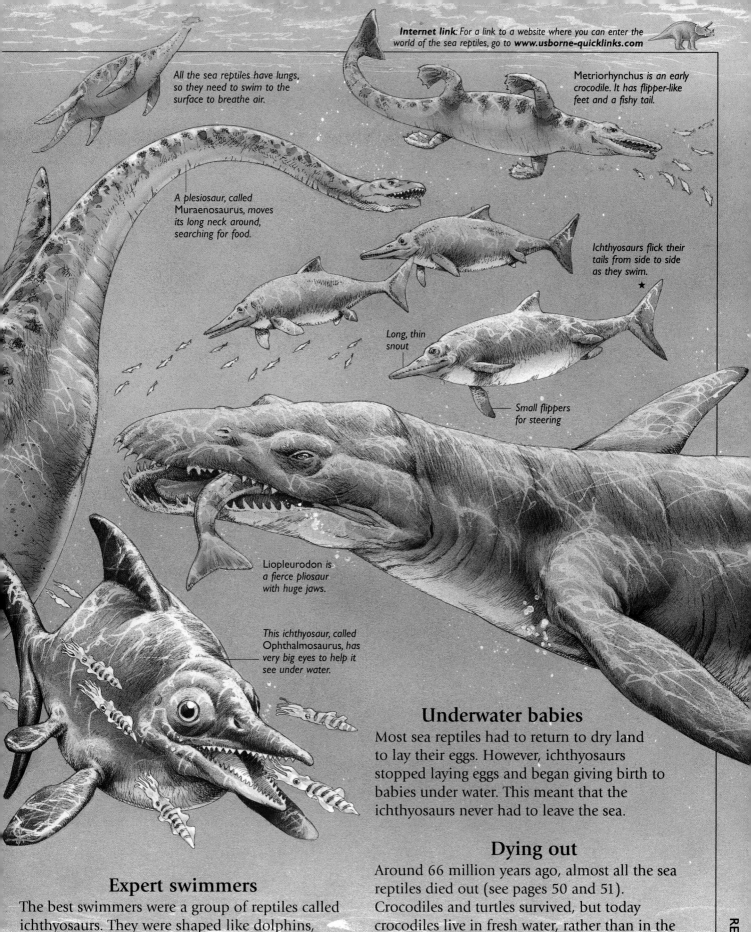

Internet link: *For a link to a website where you can enter the world of the sea reptiles, go to* **www.usborne-quicklinks.com**

All the sea reptiles have lungs, so they need to swim to the surface to breathe air.

Metriorhynchus *is an early crocodile. It has flipper-like feet and a fishy tail.*

A plesiosaur, called Muraenosaurus, *moves its long neck around, searching for food.*

Ichthyosaurs flick their tails from side to side as they swim.

★

Long, thin snout

Small flippers for steering

Liopleurodon *is a fierce pliosaur with huge jaws.*

This ichthyosaur, called Ophthalmosaurus, *has very big eyes to help it see under water.*

Underwater babies

Most sea reptiles had to return to dry land to lay their eggs. However, ichthyosaurs stopped laying eggs and began giving birth to babies under water. This meant that the ichthyosaurs never had to leave the sea.

Dying out

Around 66 million years ago, almost all the sea reptiles died out (see pages 50 and 51). Crocodiles and turtles survived, but today crocodiles live in fresh water, rather than in the sea. Turtles are the only present-day reptiles that spend their lives in the ocean.

Expert swimmers

The best swimmers were a group of reptiles called ichthyosaurs. They were shaped like dolphins, with streamlined bodies and large fins that helped them to glide swiftly through the ocean.

Flying Reptiles

Around 225 million years ago, during the Triassic Period, some reptiles evolved wings. These flying reptiles are known as pterosaurs. Pterosaurs may have evolved from tree-climbing reptiles which gradually grew wings to help them glide from branch to branch.

★ *Sharovipteryx*, an early gliding reptile, may have been an ancestor of the pterosaurs.

Flap of skin

Another idea is that pterosaurs were descended from reptiles called archosaurs (see page 35). Archosaurs ran along the ground on two legs, and some may have developed wings to help them catch flying insects.

Short-tailed insect-eaters

Near the end of the Jurassic Period, some new, short-tailed pterosaurs appeared. These pterosaurs could twist and turn in the air far more easily than their long-tailed ancestors. They probably caught fast-moving insects.

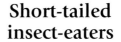
Pterodactylus slept hanging upside down.

Pterodactylus hunted insects. ★

Like all pterosaurs, Pterodactylus had excellent eyesight for spotting its prey.

Each wing was supported by a very long finger.

Leathery wing

Early flyers

By the start of the Jurassic Period, about 200 million years ago, several types of pterosaurs had appeared. They all had big, leathery wings, short necks and long, bony tails. Some of them flew over the ocean, catching fish in their pointed jaws.

Rhamphorhynchus was an early pterosaur that caught fish.

Bony tail

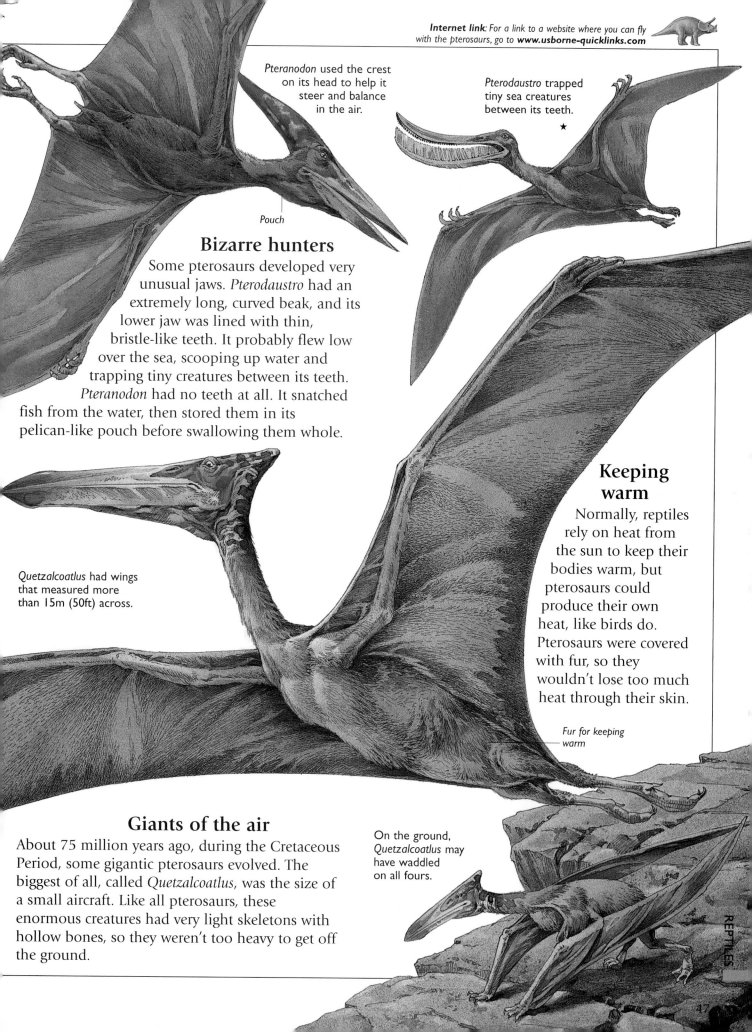

Internet link: For a link to a website where you can fly with the pterosaurs, go to **www.usborne-quicklinks.com**

Pteranodon used the crest on its head to help it steer and balance in the air.

Pouch

Pterodaustro trapped tiny sea creatures between its teeth.

★

Bizarre hunters

Some pterosaurs developed very unusual jaws. *Pterodaustro* had an extremely long, curved beak, and its lower jaw was lined with thin, bristle-like teeth. It probably flew low over the sea, scooping up water and trapping tiny creatures between its teeth. *Pteranodon* had no teeth at all. It snatched fish from the water, then stored them in its pelican-like pouch before swallowing them whole.

Quetzalcoatlus had wings that measured more than 15m (50ft) across.

Keeping warm

Normally, reptiles rely on heat from the sun to keep their bodies warm, but pterosaurs could produce their own heat, like birds do. Pterosaurs were covered with fur, so they wouldn't lose too much heat through their skin.

Fur for keeping warm

Giants of the air

About 75 million years ago, during the Cretaceous Period, some gigantic pterosaurs evolved. The biggest of all, called *Quetzalcoatlus*, was the size of a small aircraft. Like all pterosaurs, these enormous creatures had very light skeletons with hollow bones, so they weren't too heavy to get off the ground.

On the ground, *Quetzalcoatlus* may have waddled on all fours.

REPTILES

47

The First Bird

For many years, experts were not sure how birds evolved. However, they now think that birds are descended from small, meat-eating dinosaurs that ran along the ground on their back legs.

Dinosaurs and birds

Dinosaurs and birds are surprisingly similar. Dinosaurs laid eggs with hard shells, like birds do. Some even made nests, and cared for their young until they were old enough to survive on their own. Many dinosaurs had bird-like skeletons, and some had beaks.

Dinosaurs with feathers

In 1996, scientists discovered a fossil of a dinosaur called *Sinosauropteryx*. This fossil showed that *Sinosauropteryx* had a fluffy covering all over its body.

★ *Sinosauropteryx*

Other fossils have recently been found showing dinosaurs with short feathers on their bodies, tails and arms. Dinosaurs may have evolved feathers to keep themselves warm, or to attract a mate.

Caudipteryx, a feathered dinosaur

Flapping and leaping

Experts are not sure how feathered dinosaurs began to fly. They may have started flapping their arms while chasing insects, and accidentally learned to fly. Another explanation is that some dinosaurs learned to climb trees, and then began flying as they leaped between branches.

Early bird

The first true bird we know of appeared about 150 million years ago, during the Jurassic Period. It is called *Archaeopteryx*, which means "ancient feather". Although it had feathers and wings, like birds today, *Archaeopteryx* had teeth and a long, bony tail, like a dinosaur. It also had claws on its wings.

This picture shows *Archaeopteryx* in a forest.

A long tail helps to keep the bird steady in the air.

Into the air

Archaeopteryx was probably too heavy to take off from the ground. Instead, it scampered up trees, then launched itself into the air, hunting for insects. Once in the air, it could flap its wings quite powerfully. However, it may not have been able to change direction very quickly while it was flying.

This Archaeopteryx is taking off from a branch.

Strong legs and feet for running and jumping

Archaeopteryx hunts slow-moving insects, such as dragonflies.

Specially shaped feathers help the bird move smoothly through the air.

Scaly head

Archaeopteryx has pointed teeth for trapping insects.

Long claws for climbing trees

Pieces of a puzzle

Experts have known about *Archaeopteryx* since 1860, when the first fossil of this creature was found. The recent discovery that some dinosaurs had feathers has finally helped to prove the link between dinosaurs and birds.

★ Fossil of *Archaeopteryx*

REPTILES

The Death of the Dinosaurs

Around 66 million years ago, at the end of the Cretaceous Period, lots of creatures died out completely. All the dinosaurs became extinct, except for some feathered ones that had evolved into birds. Flying reptiles and most sea reptiles also died out. No one is certain why this happened, but scientists have given several different explanations.

Deadly rock?

Near the end of the Cretaceous Period, the Earth was struck by an enormous rock, or meteorite, measuring up to 10km (6 miles) across. As it hit the Earth, the meteorite would have smashed into tiny pieces, surrounding the planet in clouds of dust.

The dust clouds would have made the Earth cold and dark for months, killing off any creatures that needed warmth to survive. Without light, many plants must have died as well, leaving the animals with nothing to eat. The meteorite could also have caused massive earthquakes and giant tidal waves.

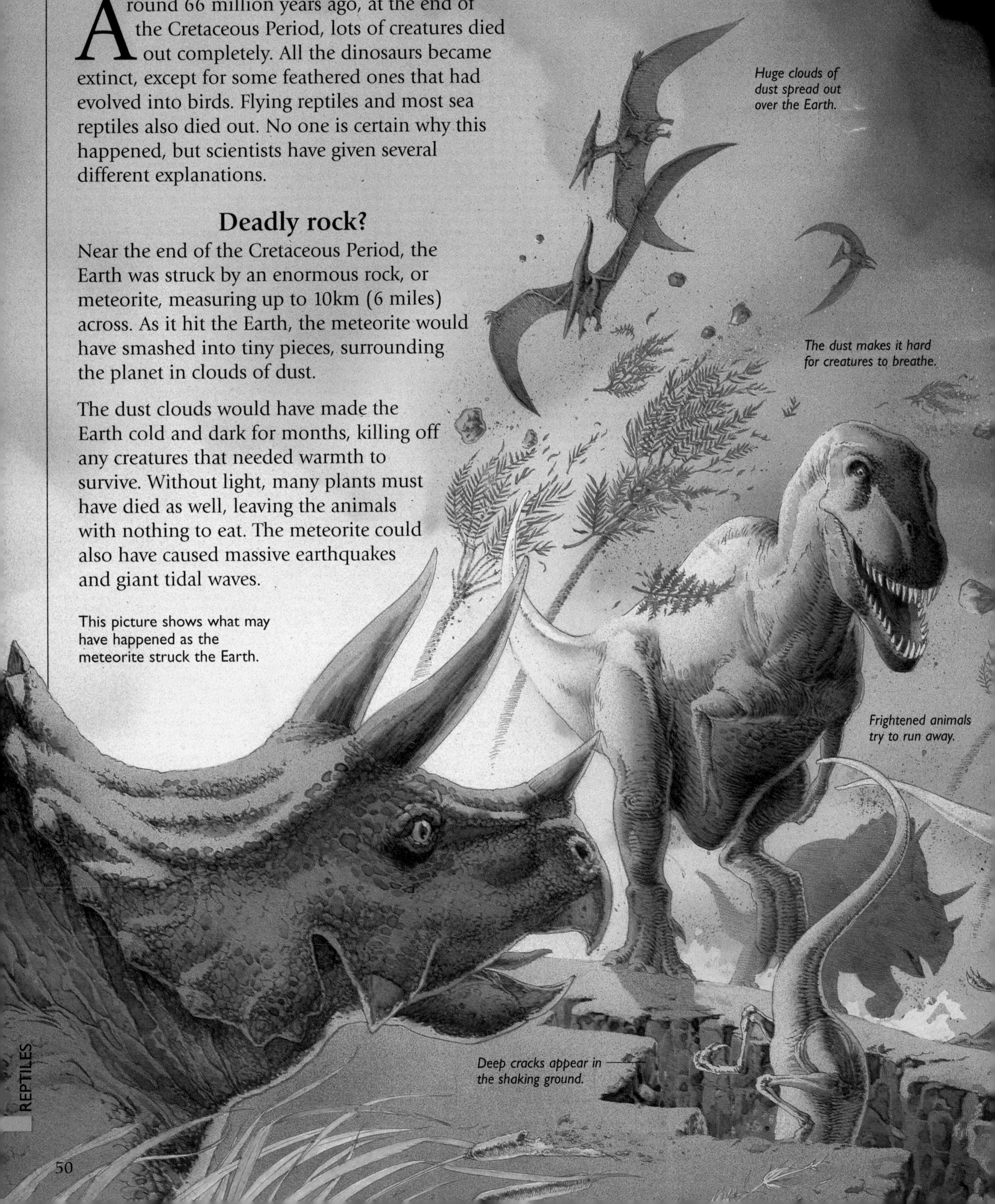

This picture shows what may have happened as the meteorite struck the Earth.

Huge clouds of dust spread out over the Earth.

The dust makes it hard for creatures to breathe.

Frightened animals try to run away.

Deep cracks appear in the shaking ground.

Lava shower?

Another explanation is that many volcanoes all over the world may have erupted at around the same time. The erupting volcanoes would have poured out vast amounts of hot lava (liquid rock) onto the Earth's surface, and sent clouds of dust and poisonous gases high into the air. These gases could also have caused harmful acid rain to fall.

Red-hot lava pouring from a volcano

Climate change?

By 66 million years ago, the weather all over the world had become cooler and more changeable. Dinosaurs relied on heat from the sun to keep themselves warm, and they may not have been able to cope with a changing climate.

Several causes

There is probably no single reason why so many animals died out. The meteorite must have killed off many creatures, but animals may also have been affected by a change in the weather.

The survivors

Mysteriously, some creatures did not die out. Some reptiles, such as lizards and snakes, survived, as well as most birds, insects and amphibians. Other survivors were a group of animals called mammals (see page 52).

Dragonfly (insect)

Some creatures that survived

Gull (bird)

Lizard (reptile)

Rat (mammal)

Frog (amphibian)

Many creatures are killed or injured by pieces of flying rock.

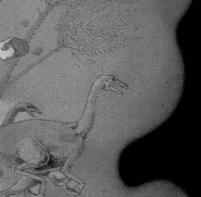

No one is sure why these animals survived, but mammals can produce their own heat, so they could have stayed warm in a cooler climate. Birds can also produce their own heat, and small reptiles, such as lizards, could have burrowed underground to keep warm.

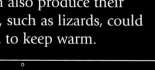
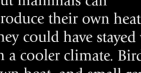

The First Mammals

Around 200 million years ago, a new group of creatures, called mammals, began to appear on the Earth. The first mammals were tiny, insect-eating animals that looked like mice or shrews.

Megazostrodon, ★
one of the first
mammals

What is a mammal?

Mammals have hair or bristles on their skin, and feed their babies with milk. Their bodies are endothermic, or warm-blooded. This means that they can produce their own heat and stay warm, even when the weather gets cold. Mammals also have several different kinds of teeth, which they use for cutting and chewing a variety of foods.

Reptile ancestors

Around 90 million years before the first mammals appeared, a group of reptiles evolved that had large heads, short legs and barrel-shaped bodies. They are known as synapsids (see pages 32 and 33).

By the start of the Triassic Period, some synapsids had become furry and had developed varied teeth. Some of them may even have been able to stay warm all the time, like mammals. Experts believe that the first mammals evolved from small, furry synapsids.

Thrinaxodon,
a furry
synapsid
the size of
a small dog
★

Living with the dinosaurs

The first mammals appeared around the same time as the first dinosaurs, but unlike the dinosaurs they did not change or develop fast. For more than 100 million years, until the dinosaurs died out, mammals stayed very small. They scurried around quietly, and usually only came out at night, when most other creatures were asleep.

This picture shows some early mammals in a forest at evening time.

The mammals try to keep
out of the dinosaurs' way.

Some plant-eating
mammals look like voles.

Mammals have
large eyes so they
can see at night.

Shrew-like
mammal

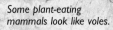

Once the sun has gone down, the dinosaurs become cold and slow.

The mammals' strong sense of smell helps them to find food in the dark.

Mammals have good hearing, so they can tell when dinosaurs are coming.

Some rat-like mammals can climb trees.

Mammals can keep themselves warm, so they can stay active at night.

Egg-laying mammals

The first mammals probably all laid eggs, like their reptile ancestors did. However, unlike reptiles, the mammals fed their young with milk. Egg-laying mammals are called monotremes. Two types of monotremes still survive in Australia and Papua New Guinea. They are the spiny anteaters and the duck-billed platypus.

Duck-billed platypus
★

MAMMALS

53

Mammals with Pouches

The first mammals probably all laid eggs (see page 53), but around 100 million years ago some mammals started giving birth to very tiny babies. The babies crawled up into a pouch on their mother's stomach and continued to grow there.

Mammals with pouches are called marsupials. Today, marsupials are found mainly in Australia, but a few species live in North and South America.

Marsupial babies

Newborn marsupials are no bigger than a bee. The baby stays in its mother's pouch and drinks milk from her nipples until it is fully developed and ready to explore the outside world.

Diagram of a kangaroo, a present-day marsupial

★

Baby

Pouch

Placentals

A few million years after the first marsupials appeared, a different kind of mammal, called a placental, evolved. Placental mothers keep their babies inside their bodies until the babies are large enough to survive on their own. Most mammals alive today are placentals.

Placental babies

Before they are born, placental babies get their food from a part of their mother's body called the placenta. After the babies are born, the mother looks after them and feeds them with milk from her nipples.

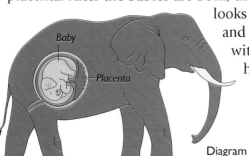

Baby

Placenta

Diagram of an elephant,
★ a present-day placental

Mammals spread out

At the time of the early mammals, the Earth's surface looked very different from the way it does today. All the continents were linked to each other, so marsupials and placentals could spread out across the world.

However, at the same time as the mammals were spreading out, the continents were very slowly drifting apart. This meant that some mammals became stranded in different parts of the world.

The marsupial Procoptodon is an ancestor of today's kangaroos.

Marsupials in Australia

Around 85,000 years ago, Australia became an island. By that time, no placentals had reached Australia, but a wide range of marsupials developed there.

This scene shows some of the marsupials that lived in Australia 10,000 years ago.

Diprotodon *digs up bushes with its paws.*

Thylacoleo *is a fierce hunter.*

Palorchestes *uses its short trunk to pull down leaves to eat.*

Procoptodon *is about 2.5m (8ft) tall.*

This young Procoptodon *is jumping into its mother's pouch for safety.*

Powerful legs for leaping

The rise of the placentals

In many parts of the world, the marsupials died out completely. This happened because placentals are generally better at surviving than marsupials. Tiny babies are safer inside their mother's body than they are in a pouch, and placentals are better at training their young to survive.

Marsupials survive

In a few parts of the world, marsupials have thrived. They have coped especially well in Australia because they are able to stop giving birth when the weather becomes too hot and dry for their young to survive. When the weather gets cooler, they start having babies again.

MAMMALS

55

The Rise of the Mammals

After the dinosaurs died out, around 66 million years ago, life became less dangerous for the mammals. They started to eat a wide range of foods and began to explore new places to live.

By 30 million years ago, a great variety of mammals had evolved. They spread out all over the world, and soon became the fastest, strongest and most intelligent group of creatures on Earth.

Rodents

Mammals with very strong teeth gnawed and nibbled at roots, bushes and tree trunks. These gnawing animals are known as rodents. Some of the early rodents looked like rats, rabbits and hares.

Palaeolagus, an early rabbit

Plant-eaters

Many early mammals ate soft plants and leaves. Most of these plant-eaters were slow-moving and clumsy, and some of them grew to be much bigger than any land mammals today.

Birbalomys, an ancestor of the guinea pig

Stylinodon, a badger-sized rodent

Uintatherium, a rhino-sized plant-eater ★

Didolodus, a pig-sized plant-eater

Tree-climbers

One group of mammals, called primates, learned to climb trees. Over millions of years, primates evolved into apes, and then into human beings. Most of the early primates looked like squirrels, monkeys and lemurs.

Smilodectes, a lemur-like primate

Branisella, an early monkey ★

Into the air

Some tree-climbing mammals grew flaps of skin between their legs so that they could glide from tree to tree. Around the same time, a group of insect-eaters gradually evolved into bats, with wings of thin skin supported by very long "fingers".

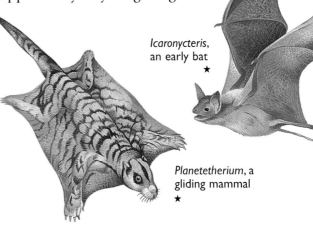

Icaronycteris, an early bat ★

Planetetherium, a gliding mammal ★

Into the oceans

A few land mammals managed to move into the oceans. They developed smooth, streamlined bodies which were suited to life in the water. Slowly, the early sea mammals evolved into whales, dolphins and seals.

Pakicetus, the earliest known whale

Meat-eaters

Some mammals ate meat, instead of plants or insects. Some of these early hunters looked like weasels and otters, and others looked like lions, wolves and bears.

Patriofelis, an early big cat ★

Cladosictis, an otter-like meat-eater

Basilosaurus, a ★ long-bodied whale

Hunters and Scavengers

Around 60 million years ago, some mammals began to hunt and eat other animals. At first, these meat-eating mammals were not very fast or clever, but gradually they evolved into expert hunters.

Early meat-eaters

The first meat-eating mammals were called creodonts. They had small brains, short legs and flat feet. This did not matter much, because the plant-eating mammals that they hunted were as unintelligent and slow-moving as they were.

This picture shows the creodont *Sarkastodon* chasing a plant-eater called *Hyrachyus*.

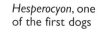

Like most creodonts, Sarkastodon cannot run very fast.

Sarkastodon's teeth are not very good at tearing up meat.

Scavengers

Some of the early meat-eaters ate dead animals that they found, instead of going hunting. Animals that do this are called scavengers. Scavengers developed special teeth for crushing bones, so that they could eat the soft bone marrow inside.

Hyaenodon scavenging meat from a dead animal

★

Better hunters

Gradually, some plant-eating mammals became very good at running and started to live in herds (see pages 60 and 61). This meant that the animals that hunted them had to change too.

Hesperocyon, one of the first dogs

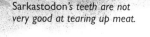

Cerdocyon, an ancestor of the fox

A new group of meat-eating mammals evolved that were fast-moving, powerful and cunning. These mammals, known as carnivores, had excellent hearing and eyesight, and a strong sense of smell. Today's dogs and cats are descended from these early carnivores.

Homotherium, an early cat

Dinofelis, a panther-like cat

MAMMALS

Hunting in teams

Around six million years ago, early dogs and wolves began to hunt in teams, or packs. This meant that they could hunt animals much larger than themselves. Some big cats, such as lions, also hunted in teams.

Today, wolves still hunt together in packs. These wolves are howling to other members of their pack to show that they are ready to start hunting.

Chasing and stalking

Dogs chased after their prey until the hunted animals were exhausted, but cats hunted in a different way. First, they stalked their prey (followed it very quietly), and then they pounced on it swiftly and suddenly.

Teeth and claws

Carnivores developed sharp claws for holding their prey, and long, pointed teeth for tearing up meat. Some big cats, known as sabre-toothed cats, had incredibly long, blade-like teeth, or fangs.

In this scene, a sabre-toothed cat, called *Smilodon*, is stalking its prey. ★

Powerful neck and shoulders

Smilodon *uses its curved fangs for stabbing its prey and tearing up meat.*

Another cat prowls through the long grass.

Smilodon *pads very quietly on its soft paws.*

Sharp claws for grasping prey

Plant-eaters' Problems

The first plant-eating mammals (or herbivores) were slow-moving creatures with small brains. Most of them were the size of today's pigs or badgers, but a few were incredibly tall and heavy.

This is *Indricotherium*, the largest mammal that ever lived on land. ★

Tough, leathery skin

Indricotherium *munches leaves from the tops of trees.*

Indricotherium *is 8m (26ft) tall and weighs as much as four elephants.*

The growth of the grasslands

Around 40 million years ago, the weather all over the world began to get cooler. Gradually, most of the tropical forests were replaced by grassy plains. The herbivores were forced to eat grass, which is tough to chew and hard to digest, and many animals died out because they couldn't cope with their new food.

Eating grass

Slowly, new kinds of herbivores evolved that were able to eat grass. Animals that eat grass are known as grazers. They have flat teeth with ridges that are very good at grinding. Grazers chew and swallow their food several times, bringing partly digested food back up into their mouths, so that they can chew it again. This repeated chewing of food is known as "chewing the cud".

Horns and tusks

The early herbivores wandered through forests nibbling leaves and plants. They were hunted by meat-eating mammals, and some of them developed strange-looking horns and tusks to defend themselves against predators (hunters).

Brontotherium had two huge horns on its nose. ★

Roaming the plains

The grasslands provided plenty of food and the number of grazers increased rapidly. By 25 million years ago, the first deer, cattle, sheep and antelope had all appeared on the plains. They lived in large groups, or herds, that roamed over the grasslands.

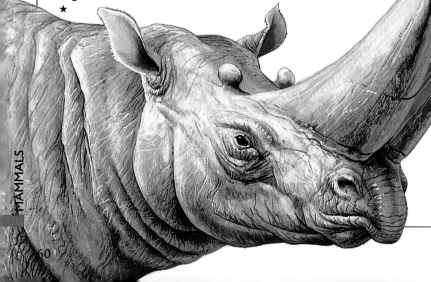

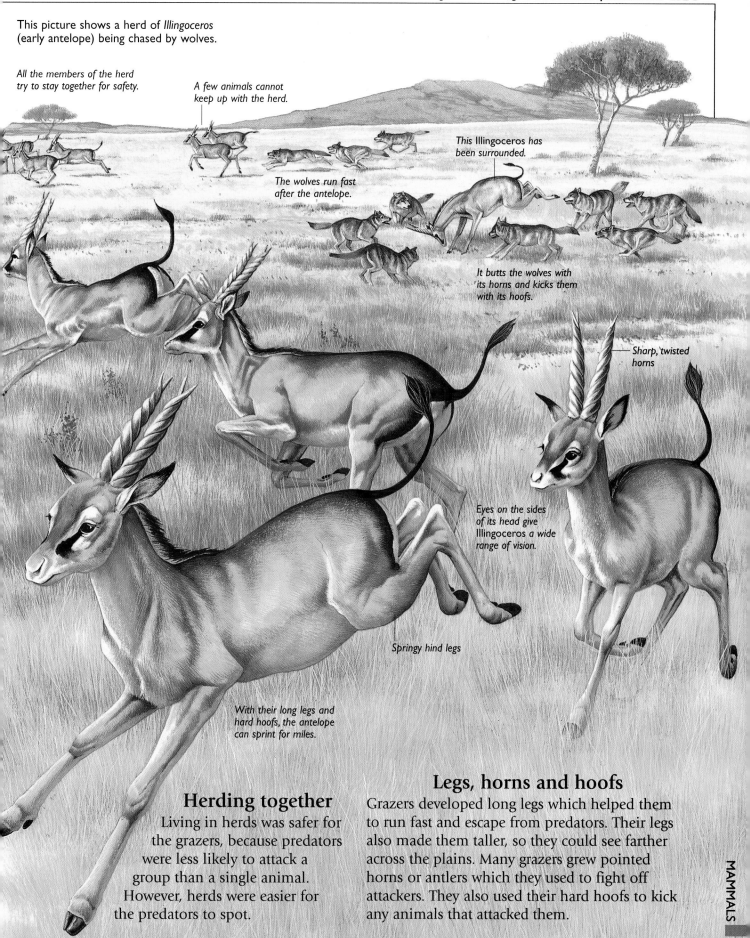

This picture shows a herd of *Illingoceros* (early antelope) being chased by wolves.

All the members of the herd try to stay together for safety.

A few animals cannot keep up with the herd.

The wolves run fast after the antelope.

This Illingoceros has been surrounded.

It butts the wolves with its horns and kicks them with its hoofs.

Sharp, twisted horns

Eyes on the sides of its head give Illingoceros a wide range of vision.

Springy hind legs

With their long legs and hard hoofs, the antelope can sprint for miles.

Herding together

Living in herds was safer for the grazers, because predators were less likely to attack a group than a single animal. However, herds were easier for the predators to spot.

Legs, horns and hoofs

Grazers developed long legs which helped them to run fast and escape from predators. Their legs also made them taller, so they could see farther across the plains. Many grazers grew pointed horns or antlers which they used to fight off attackers. They also used their hard hoofs to kick any animals that attacked them.

MAMMALS

61

The Horse's Tale

The first horses lived around 50 million years ago, when the Earth was covered with forests. They were much smaller than horses today (about the size of a small dog) and they wandered through the forests, nibbling soft leaves. Sometimes, the horses were attacked by vicious giant birds.

This picture shows a giant bird, called *Diatryma*, chasing *Hyracotherium*, the earliest known species of horse. ★

Disappearing forests

Gradually, the forests where the early horses lived were replaced by vast, grassy plains (see page 60). This meant that the horses had to change in order to survive.

Bigger and faster

By 35 million years ago, horses had grown longer legs for running on the plains, and had developed stronger teeth for chewing tough grass. They also lost a toe from each of their front feet and began to run on their strong middle toes. This new way of running made them lighter on their feet.

Diatryma is a powerful runner, but it can't fly.

Diatryma is 2m (6ft) tall.

Hyracotherium is only 40cm (15in) tall.

Short neck

Small, blunt teeth

Hyracotherium has four toes on its front feet and three toes on its hind feet.

The horse's toes spread out to stop it from sinking into soft ground.

Living on the plains

By around 10 million years ago, horses had grown to the size of small ponies. They lived in herds on the open plains and were very good at chewing and digesting grass. The horses had to run very fast to escape from wild cats and dogs, but they could also use their hoofs to fight off attackers.

A group of *Merychippus* (early horses) on the plains

The pattern on the horses' coats makes them hard to spot in long grass.

Sometimes, two males fight each other to see which one is stronger.

Long, powerful neck

These horses have sharp front teeth for cutting grass, and strong back teeth for chewing it.

Very small side toes

Strong middle toe capped with a tough hoof

Long, slender legs for running fast

A new kind of horse

About five million years ago, a new kind of horse, called *Equus*, appeared in North America. These horses were larger than *Merychippus* and each of their feet had a single, hoof-covered toe. They spread from America to Asia and Europe, and eventually to Africa and India. *Equus* is the only kind of horse living in the world today.

These pictures show how horses evolved over 45 million years. ★

Hyracotherium
(50 million years ago)

Mesohippus
(35 million years ago)

Merychippus
(10 million years ago)

Equus (5 million years ago)

MAMMALS

63

Animals of South America

Around 50 million years after the first mammals appeared, the area of land that is now South America became cut off from North America.

Even though the mammals of South America developed completely separately from any other animals, many of them looked like mammals from other parts of the world. This is because creatures evolve to suit their surroundings, so animals living in the same kind of surroundings tend to evolve in a similar way.

Thomashuxleya looked like a warthog.

Diadiaphorus looked like a horse.

★ *Macrauchenia* had a camel-like body and a short trunk.

Mammals with pouches

A wide range of marsupials (mammals with pouches) evolved in South America, although almost no marsupials live there today. Most of these creatures were hunters and many of them looked like meat-eating mammals from other parts of the world.

Theosodon was an ancestor of the llama.

Toxodon looked like a hippo.

Argyrolagus was a marsupial that looked like a kangaroo rat.

Plant-eaters and gnawers

As well as the marsupials, many kinds of placental mammals (see page 54) developed in South America. These animals ate soft plants and grasses or gnawed at roots and branches. Most of them looked like plant-eaters or rodents (gnawers) from other parts of the world, but a few, like *Macrauchenia*, were very unusual.

Thylacosmilus was a marsupial that looked like a big cat.

Protypotherium looked like a rabbit.

Strange creatures

Two kinds of South American mammals were completely different from any other animals in the world. These were the sloths and the glyptodonts. Sloths had long, thick hair and moved extremely slowly, and glyptodonts had a bony dome on their backs to protect them.

Changing places

Around five million years ago, North and South America became joined by a bridge of land. Some South American mammals, such as sloths, glyptodonts and porcupines, began to move north, while northern mammals, such as rabbits, horses and big cats, began spreading south.

The North American porcupine originally came from South America.

★ *Megatherium* was a giant sloth that lived on the ground.

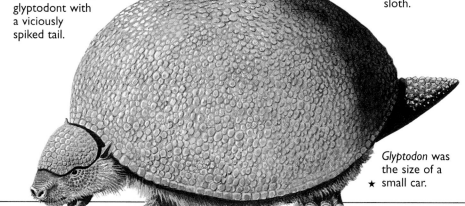

Daedicurus was a glyptodont with a viciously spiked tail.

Hapalops was a tree-climbing sloth.

Glyptodon was the size of a
★ small car.

Dying out

Not long after North and South America became joined, many species of South American mammals died out. Experts used to think that this happened because the mammals of the south could not compete with the northern mammals. However, many southern species were already disappearing by the time the northern mammals arrived in the south.

Changes in the weather

No one knows why so many South American mammals became extinct. However, around the time that North and South America joined together, the weather all over the world became very changeable. Some southern mammals may have died out because, unlike the mammals of the north, they were not used to changes in their climate.

MAMMALS

65

The Elephant's Story

The earliest ancestors of today's elephants were long-bodied, pig-like creatures that lived in the swamps of Africa around 40 million years ago. They wallowed around in the water, feeding on soft-leaved plants.

The early elephant *Moeritherium* spent most of its life in the water.

Extraordinary elephants

Many different kinds of elephants evolved in Africa, Asia, Europe and America, and some of them had teeth, tusks and trunks that grew in strange shapes. However, around five million years ago, an elephant called *Stegodon* evolved which looked very similar to elephants today.

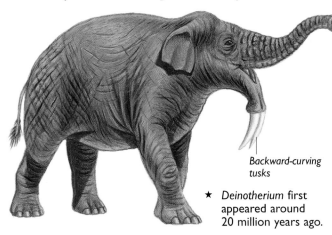

Backward-curving tusks

★ *Deinotherium* first appeared around 20 million years ago.

Trunks and tusks

Over millions of years, the early elephants became taller. This made it hard for them to reach down to the plants that they ate. Gradually, their upper lips and noses grew longer and developed into a short trunk.

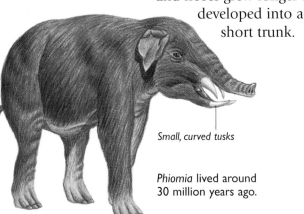

Small, curved tusks

Phiomia lived around 30 million years ago.

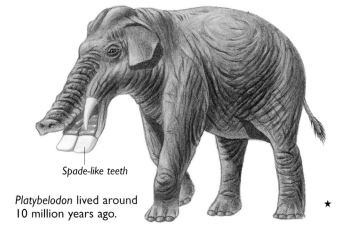

Spade-like teeth

Platybelodon lived around 10 million years ago. ★

Stegodon evolved around 5 million years ago. ★

The elephants used their trunks to suck up water and shovel plants into their mouths. They also grew curved tusks which helped them to scoop up their food.

Mammoths drowned in tar

Around two million years ago, a group of enormous elephants, called mammoths, appeared. Mammoths measured up to 4.5m (15ft) tall, and had very long, curved tusks.

Fossils of mammoths and other animals have been found at La Brea, near Los Angeles in the USA. Around 15,000 years ago, there were several pits filled with tar in this area. The tar became covered with rainwater, and many animals thought the pits were drinking pools. Hundreds of creatures became stuck in the tar and drowned.

Vulture

Wolves and wild cats feed on any animals that have drowned.

Mammoths come to the pool to drink.

This picture shows a tar pit at La Brea.

Elephant ancestors

Around 10,000 years ago, the mammoths died out. This may have happened because the weather became too warm for them or because they were hunted by humans. Two groups of elephants survived in Africa and Asia. They were the ancestors of today's elephants.

African elephants like these are descended from elephants that lived in Africa about four million years ago.

MAMMALS

67

Animals of the Ice Age

Several times in the history of the Earth, large parts of the world have been buried under thick sheets of ice. Each time, the ice has stayed frozen for thousands of years, and these long, freezing periods are known as ice ages.

The last ice age

The last ice age began around 100,000 years ago and ended around 10,000 years ago. During this time, large areas of land in the northern half of the world were covered in ice.

This map shows the world during the last ice age.

■ Areas covered in ice
■ Frozen lands where animals could live

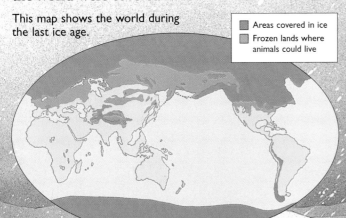

Frozen mammoths

Sometimes, animals fell into ponds which later froze solid. The animals' bodies were trapped in ice and could not rot away, so they were preserved for thousands of years. Several woolly mammoths have been found in the ice of Siberia, in northern Russia. Some of these mammoths were covered with hair, and some still had their last meal preserved in their stomachs.

This baby mammoth was discovered in the ice of Siberia in 1977.

Woolly mammoths

Living on the edge

At the start of the last ice age, many animals moved to warmer areas, but some stayed in the frozen lands near the edge of the ice sheets. Very cold places where the ground is always frozen are known as tundra. The animals of the tundra grew thick coats to keep themselves warm. Most of them ate mosses, lichens and small bushes, but some were hunters.

This scene shows some of the animals that lived in the tundra.

The Arctic hare's white coat helps it to hide in the snow.

The Arctic fox is a cunning hunter.

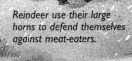

Reindeer use their large horns to defend themselves against meat-eaters.

Between the ice ages

The last ice age was one of a series of ice ages that began two million years ago. In between these freezing periods, the weather became very warm. Thick forests grew where the ice sheets had been, and animals that were used to the cold were forced to travel to cooler areas. Meanwhile, heat-loving animals, such as hippos and lions, were able to live in places as far north as Europe and North America.

Disappearing animals

At the end of the last ice age, around 10,000 years ago, many animals died out. No one knows exactly why this happened, but one reason must have been the change in the weather. Some animals, such as mammoths, were hunted by early humans, and this could be another reason why they disappeared.

Icy winds whistle across the tundra.

The woolly rhinoceros is covered with thick hair.

Lichens and mosses grow on rocks.

Bears shelter in caves when the weather becomes very cold.

Musk oxen roam the tundra, searching for plants to eat.

Small plants and bushes poke up through the snow.

MAMMALS

Apes and Monkeys

Apes, monkeys and humans all belong to a group of mammals known as primates. The first primates appeared on the Earth about 66 million years ago. They were small, squirrel-like creatures that scurried around in the trees.

Plesiadapis, an early primate ★

Sharp claws

This picture shows monkeys and apes in a forest around 14 million years ago.

Mesopithecus monkeys live in the treetops.

This monkey is teaching its young to climb.

Gigantopithecus is an enormous ape. It is around 2.5m (8ft) tall.

Fingers and toes

Gradually, some early primates began to change. Instead of claws, they grew fingers and toes with sensitive tips. Fingers and toes were useful for judging the thickness of branches and for holding onto them tightly.

Gigantopithecus lives on the forest floor. It is too heavy to climb trees.

Seeing in 3-D

Primates developed much better eyesight than most other mammals. Each of their eyes saw a different picture, and their brains put the pictures together to make a three-dimensional image. Seeing in 3-D helped primates to judge distances when they leaped from one branch to another.

Early monkeys and apes

By around 30 million years ago, some primates had evolved into the first monkeys and apes. Even the earliest monkeys were expert tree-climbers, and some monkeys developed long, curling tails for grasping branches. Apes were bigger and stronger than monkeys. They had broad chests, flexible shoulders and strong arms, which helped them to swing from tree to tree.

Learning to survive

Climbing and balancing are difficult things to do, and apes and monkeys evolved big brains to help them cope with life in the trees. They began to live in large groups, and to look after each other. They also spent a long time bringing up their babies and teaching them how to survive.

This monkey is cleaning another monkey's fur. This is called grooming.

This Dryopithecus ape is using its strong arms to swing between branches.

On the ground, Dryopithecus walks on all fours.

Climbing and walking

Over millions of years, different apes and monkeys learned to live in different parts of the trees, so that they could all find enough food to eat. Some even left the trees and started living on the ground.

When they were on the ground, some apes sometimes walked on two feet instead of crawling on all fours. This left their hands free for carrying food. However, they couldn't stand up straight, which made it hard to walk very far on two feet.

Monkeys and apes use their fingers and thumbs to make a tight grip.

This ape, called Ramapithecus, may have been able to walk for short distances on two feet.

Ramapithecus uses its hands to carry food.

Changing faces

Most early primates had long noses, or snouts, for sniffing out their food, and long, pointed teeth for nibbling fruit and insects. However, some later apes relied on their eyes instead of their noses to find food, so their snouts gradually became shorter. Their teeth also became shorter and flatter, so they could grind up the tough plants and grasses that grew on the ground.

HUMANS

71

Southern Apes

The footprints at Laetoli

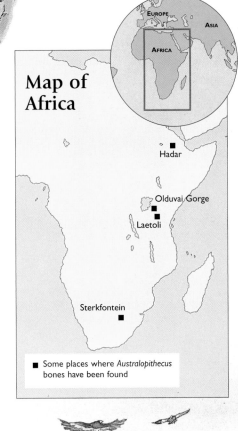

Map of Africa

Hadar

Olduvai Gorge

Laetoli

Sterkfontein

■ Some places where *Australopithecus* bones have been found

Over five million years ago, some apes in Africa started learning to walk upright. Apes that walk upright are called hominids. We are hominids too, but the earliest ones were very different from us. They were much shorter than us, and had small brains and apelike faces.

The earliest known hominid is called *Australopithecus*, which means "southern ape". It lived from around five million to a million years ago.

Australopithecus skull

Experts dig up new hominid bones all the time. The most famous set of bones is an *Australopithecus* skeleton from Hadar, in Ethiopia. The skeleton has been named "Lucy".

Finding footprints

At Laetoli, in Tanzania, experts have found a trail of *Australopithecus* footprints preserved in volcanic ash. This proves that Lucy and her friends had started walking upright.

Swinging through trees

At first, *Australopithecus* spent a lot of time in the trees. It had long, curved fingers and toes, and long arms, which helped it to grip branches and swing between them. However, its knees were like ours, which shows that it could also walk upright.

This picture shows a group of early *Australopithecus*.

The group lives at the edge of a thick forest.

Most Australopithecus are less than 1.5m (5ft) tall.

Walking on two feet leaves the hands free for carrying things.

Stones are useful for cracking open tough-skinned fruit.

Australopithecus has a hairy body and an apelike face.

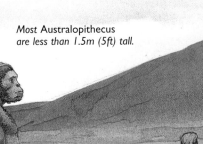

Internet link: For a link to a website where you can see how experts learned about Australopithecus from its bones, go to **www.usborne-quicklinks.com**

Why did apes stand up?

Nobody is sure why some apes began walking upright, but one explanation is the weather.

Between seven and four million years ago, the Earth's climate got much cooler. In East Africa, the forests where *Australopithecus* lived began to disappear. It was harder to find fruit and leaves to eat, so *Australopithecus* had to travel farther to find food. Using two legs was less tiring than using four.

Standing upright also made it easier for *Australopithecus* to spot dangerous animals in the tall grass at the edge of the forest.

Different types

Eventually, *Australopithecus* seems to have evolved into several different types. Some are known as "gracile" (slender), while others are known as "robust" (large and strong). The "robust" *Australopithecus* had very powerful jaws, which allowed it to eat tough grasses and roots.

Some of the group are eating leaves and fruit from the trees.

Beyond the forest are large areas of grassland, called savannah.

Long, powerful arms

Long, curved toes and fingers for grasping branches

Standing upright, Australopithecus can see a wild cat lying in wait.

This group of Australopithecus has walked across the grassland to find food.

Some of the group use sticks to break open a termites' nest, so they can eat the insects.

HUMANS

The Tool-makers

round two and a half million years ago, a new species of hominid, called *Homo habilis*, evolved in Africa. For more than a million years, it lived alongside *Australopithecus* (see pages 72 and 73).

Homo habilis had a bigger brain than *Australopithecus*, and was more skilled. (Its name means "skilled man" in Latin.) It is sometimes known as "handy man" and is often thought of as the first human.

New skills

Australopithecus picked up sticks and stones and used them as tools, but *Homo habilis* could make its own tools. It made thin stone tools (called flakes) for cutting, and larger ones (called choppers) for smashing hard objects, such as nuts. These tools were made from flint, which is easy to shape.

★ Chopper

★ Flake

Shaping stones

Homo habilis made its tools by striking two rocks together. A long thin stone, called a hammerstone, was used to chip sharp flakes from a larger stone. This is known as stone knapping.

A group of *Homo habilis* making ★ and using tools

Chipping flakes from a stone

Hammerstone

Flake

Cracking nuts with a chopper

Sharpening sticks

Homo habilis probably made a wooden tool, called a digging stick, by sharpening one end of a branch with a stone flake. It may have used the sharpened sticks to dig up roots to eat.

Sharpening a stick with a stone flake

Digging for roots with a sharpened stick

Stealing meat

Although *Homo habilis* probably did no hunting, it did eat meat. Groups of *Homo habilis* used sharp stone tools to remove meat from the bodies of dead animals that they found. Their tools helped them to work fast, so they could get away before any wild animals attacked them.

A group of Australopithecus feeds on leaves. They cannot make tools for cutting meat.

This picture shows a group of *Homo habilis* stripping meat from a dead elephant.

These lions are coming to find food.

Large, sharp choppers are useful for smashing bone, to get at the soft marrow inside.

Stone flakes are used for slicing through meat.

The elephant died of old age.

Vultures peck at the meat.

This Homo habilis is taking away some meat to eat.

Starting to wander

Eating meat allowed *Homo habilis* to travel farther than *Australopithecus*. Because it no longer had to live so close to plants and fruit, it could explore wider areas. Its new diet also gave it more energy and helped its brain grow bigger.

HUMANS

75

The Coming of Fire

A million years after *Homo habilis* appeared (see page 74), a new hominid with an even bigger brain evolved in Africa. This species walked completely upright and is known as *Homo erectus*, which means "upright man" in Latin. *Homo erectus* people learned how to use fire, which gave them much more control over their lives.

Finding fire

Homo erectus people probably could not light fires themselves. Instead, they may have found fires that had started when lightning struck dry grass. They probably carried a burning branch away to a cave or a camp, then kept the same fire burning for days, or even weeks.

This picture shows *Homo erectus* people using fire in their cave.

Outside it is dark and cold.

Lightning has started a fire on the grassland.

People use burning branches to drive away wild animals.

These men have brought some meat to cook on the fire.

The wild cats are frightened of the fire.

Safe and warm

Fire kept *Homo erectus* people warm at night. It could also be used as a weapon against dangerous animals, which were scared away by the blaze.

Cooking food

Homo erectus people discovered that meat and plants were tastier when they were heated, and they began to cook their food. Cooked food is easier to chew, so their teeth and jaws gradually became smaller. As they ate more meat, their bodies grew stronger and taller, and their brains became bigger.

Lighting the darkness

By keeping a fire burning, *Homo erectus* people could see clearly after it got dark. This meant that, unlike earlier hominids, they did not have to go to sleep when the sun went down, but could continue working at night.

Better tools

Homo erectus people used fire to make better tools. They hardened the ends of wooden spears by holding them in the flames, and heated stones to make them easier to shape. They made the heated stones into tools called hand axes, which had very sharp edges.

★
Hand axe

People can work at night using the light of the fire.

People keep warm by the fire.

This woman is cooking meat.

This man is keeping the fire going with branches.

These plants have been cooked in the fire.

People use hand axes for cutting up meat.

Wooden spears hardening in the fire.

This woman is pushing a rock into the fire. Heated rocks are easier to shape.

Making homes

A fire provided a place where *Homo erectus* people could gather. They could make a safe home around a fire anywhere, and so they began to settle in lots of different places. Gradually, they spread out farther and farther from Africa (see page 78).

The First Explorers

For over three million years, hominids lived only in eastern and southern Africa. This changed around 1.8 million years ago, when *Homo erectus* people began to move into new areas.

Out of Africa

Gradually, *Homo erectus* people spread out, until they had explored most of Africa. Some groups moved slowly east and eventually reached Indonesia and China.

Life in a Chinese cave

One group settled in a large cave near Zhoukoudian, in China. *Homo erectus* people lived there for 250,000 years.

This scene shows *Homo erectus* people in the Zhoukoudian cave.
★

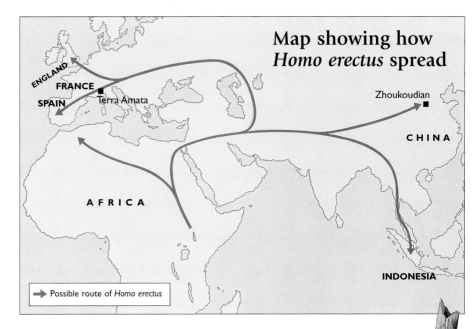

Map showing how *Homo erectus* spread

ENGLAND
FRANCE
SPAIN
Terra Amata

Zhoukoudian

CHINA

AFRICA

INDONESIA

Possible route of *Homo erectus*

Skulls and antlers

The people at Zhoukoudian ate meat from deer and horses, which they may have hunted. They made stone tools by hammering rocks with deer antlers, and also made drinking bowls from deer skulls.

★
Bowl made from a deer skull

★
Part of a deer antler used as a hammer

Discovering Europe

Homo erectus people probably arrived in Europe about 500,000 years ago. They moved around from place to place, hunting, fishing and gathering plants to eat. Eventually, they reached as far west as Spain and as far north as England.

Animal skins keep people warm outside.

Firewood

This man is using a deer antler as a hammer.

This man is shaping a deer skull into a drinking bowl.

This girl is drinking water from a deer skull.

Life on the coast

Some groups of *Homo erectus* people returned each year to stay in the same place. One group stayed every spring at a place called Terra Amata, on the south coast of France, where they may have built shelters from branches. They used wooden spears to hunt animals and catch fish.

This picture shows *Homo erectus* people hunting deer at Terra Amata.

Using fire

Homo erectus people could use fire to keep themselves warm. This meant they could move out of Africa, and into cooler areas. Their fires also kept wild animals away, so fewer people were killed, and their numbers started to grow.

Why did they travel?

Experts think that *Homo erectus* people had to travel to find enough food, because there were more people to feed. They hunted wandering animals, and the animals may have led them to new places.

People stay near streams, where they can find fresh water to drink.

Catching fish

Fish and meat are cooked on the fire.

Hunters use wooden spears and sharpened rocks.

HUMANS

Hunters of the Ice Age

Around 200,000 years ago, a new kind of people started to evolve from *Homo erectus*. These new people had bigger brains than earlier people, and are known as *Homo sapiens*, which means "wise man" in Latin.

The Neanderthal people were an early type of *Homo sapiens*. They are named after the Neander Valley in Germany, where their bones were first found. Neanderthals appeared in Europe and western Asia during an ice age, when a large part of the Earth was covered in ice and snow (see page 68).

Big and clever

For a long time, people thought Neanderthals were unintelligent, apelike creatures, but experts now think differently. Neanderthals had strong, muscular bodies and a ridge of bone above their eyes, but otherwise they were very like us. Some of them had brains that were bigger than ours.

Finding food

In the long, frozen winters of the ice age, it was hard to find plants to eat, so Neanderthals ate a lot of meat. They stripped meat from dead animals that they found, and they also hunted animals, such as horses and reindeer.

Hunting with fire

Mammoths and rhinos were too dangerous to approach but, like all animals, they were scared of fire. Sometimes, Neanderthal hunters chased these huge animals with burning branches and forced them over the edge of a cliff. The animals were killed, and the hunters could then remove the meat from the dead bodies.

This scene shows Neanderthal hunters chasing mammoths over a cliff.

The hunters shout and wave their arms to frighten the mammoths.

Ridge of bone

Large jaw

Short, stocky body

Wooden spear

Burning branches

Knotted animal skins

The Neanderthals' strong bodies help them to cope with the cold.

This man has been wounded by a mammoth.

Keeping warm

During the freezing winters, Neanderthals needed warm clothes to keep out the cold. They probably made simple tunics by knotting animal skins together. Neanderthals often sheltered in caves, but out in the open they may have made shelters from branches and animal skins.

The mammoths are terrified by the fire and the men's shouts.

New tools

Neanderthals made better tools than earlier people. They had different tools for hunting, cutting food, and shaping wood. They also used their powerful jaws as extra tools, for tearing meat from animal bones and for cleaning animal skins.

Early Families

Neanderthals were more intelligent than earlier people, and they developed a more organized way of life. This helped them to survive in the freezing cold of the ice age. They worked together in family groups and cared for anyone in their family who was sick or injured.

Helping the injured

Hunting wild animals was very dangerous, and injuries were common. Some men were so badly hurt that they could never hunt again. These men were probably looked after by their families for the rest of their lives.

Gifts for the dead?

Some experts think that the Neanderthals believed in life after death. Animal horns, stone tools and pollen from flowers have all been found in Neanderthal graves. These objects may have been placed in the graves as gifts to help dead people in the afterlife.

In this picture, a dead Neanderthal is being buried by his family and friends.

The man is buried near the back of a cave.

Deer antler to place in the grave

These people are placing gifts around the body.

Goat's horn

Flowers

This injured man is being helped by his brother.

Stone tools

Deer bones

The man's family have curled up his body.

Later, people will cover the body with soil.

Burying the dead

Neanderthals were the first people to bury their dead, instead of just leaving the bodies to decay. They dug a hole with sharpened sticks and stones, then laid the body carefully inside it.

Starting to talk?

No one really knows when people started speaking, but some experts think that Neanderthals were the first people who learned how to talk. They probably only used simple words, with lots of hand signals as well. Being able to communicate helped the Neanderthals to work together and to organize hunts. They were also able to warn each other of danger.

This scene shows Neanderthals running to warn their family that wolves are approaching.

Lots of people gather to bury the man.

The end of the Neanderthals

Around 40,000 years ago, the Neanderthals began to die out. A new type of people, who were very good at hunting, had appeared in Europe and Asia (see pages 84 to 87).

The new hunters gradually drove the Neanderthals away from the best hunting areas. Many Neanderthals starved to death, and others became weak and died of illnesses. By 30,000 years ago, they had died out completely.

The First Modern People

Around 150,000 years ago, a new type of *Homo sapiens* evolved. This species, known as *Homo sapiens sapiens*, is the one that all human beings belong to today. All modern people have a large, rounded skull, a straight forehead and a small jaw.

Skull of *Homo sapiens sapiens*
★

Hunting and gathering

The first modern people lived by hunting animals and gathering plants to eat. They kept moving from one place to another to find food. People who live like this are called hunter-gatherers. Some hunter-gatherers returned to the same place at the same time each year, and stayed there until the food ran out, before moving on.

Working together

These early people could talk just as well as people can today. Talking helped them to work together in big groups, or tribes. Each tribe probably had a leader who organized hunts.

This scene shows how a tribe of people may have lived 40,000 years ago.

These people are using slings to kill sea birds. ∧

Seal hunters

These people are collecting mussels and crabs to eat.

This boy is cleaning an animal skin with a stone scraper.

This man is telling some children about his hunting adventures.

This woman is sewing animal-skin clothes with a bone needle.

Tools with handles

By 40,000 years ago, people were making tools with handles. They made spears by fitting sharp stone blades into long sticks. They also carved pieces of bone into jagged blades and tied them to sticks, to make harpoons. Bone was used to make fish-hooks as well.

These hunters are bringing back some antelope they have caught.

Shelter made from branches and deer skins

This woman is making a basket from reeds.

Meat hanging up to dry

Dried meat can be stored for a long time without going bad.

Harpoons for catching fish and seals

Bone blade

These men are from a different tribe. They have come to trade stone blades for seashells.

Sewing clothes

People began to sew animal skins together to make clothes. They made needles from bone, and used thin strips of leather as thread.

Trading and talking

As they wandered from place to place, tribes of people traded tools and valuable objects with each other. People from different tribes told each other about their experiences and passed on information about new places.

The spirit world

People seem to have believed that the world was controlled by powerful spirits, or gods. They probably tried to contact these gods by holding religious ceremonies. Perhaps they asked the gods to help them with their hunting, or to protect dead people in the afterlife?

HUMANS

New Worlds

Modern people evolved from an earlier type of people known as *Homo erectus* (see pages 76 to 79). Some experts believe that these new people evolved in several places at roughly the same time. But many other experts think that modern people first appeared in Africa, then spread out slowly across the rest of the world.

Spreading out

Modern people probably began to travel beyond Africa to Europe and Asia around 100,000 years ago. Gradually, they replaced the earlier people that lived in these places, and by about 30,000 years ago, they were the only humans left on Earth.

Across the sea

Around 50,000 years ago, during the last ice age, groups of people set off in boats from Southeast Asia. Nobody knows why they did this. They may have been searching for food, or for more land, or perhaps they were just exploring.

This picture shows people from Southeast Asia on a voyage to find new land.

Following herds

Some tribes of people in Europe and Asia hunted wandering herds of animals, such as reindeer or bison. They followed the herds all through the year, and the animals led them to new places.

Bison

The first Americans

At times, the sea level was so low that Asia and North America were connected by a stretch of dry land, called Beringia. Herds of animals wandered across Beringia, to and from Asia and North America.

Some time between 30,000 and 12,000 years ago, tribes of people followed the herds from Asia into North America. These hunters gradually moved south until they had occupied all of North and South America.

Wooden paddle

Finding Australia

During the ice age, the sea level was much lower than it is today. This meant that there were lots of little islands where voyagers could stop and rest. However, they still had to cross miles of water between islands, and many people must have been lost at sea. Eventually, some voyagers reached the shores of Australia. They were the first people who ever lived there.

Some of the boats are made from bamboo stems tied together with thin strips of bamboo.

HUMANS

ARCTIC OCEAN

BERINGIA

ATLANTIC
OCEAN

EUROPE
40,000 years ago

ASIA
80,000 years ago

**NORTH
AMERICA**
30,000 - 12,000
years ago

ATLANTIC
OCEAN

AFRICA
150,000 - 100,000
years ago

PACIFIC OCEAN

INDIAN
OCEAN

**SOUTH
AMERICA**
Date
uncertain

AUSTRALIA
50,000 years ago

Map showing the spread of modern people

The map shows when people may have arrived
in different places.

☐ Dry land at the time of the last ice age

➔ Possible route

*Some people have
stayed behind to settle
on this island.*

*Canoes made from
hollowed-out tree trunks are
used for short journeys.*

*These people have just set
out from an island where
they spent the night.*

*Leather bag
filled with food*

HUMANS

The Mammoth-hunters

Around 30,000 years ago, during the last ice age, tribes of people arrived on the freezing plains of eastern Europe. These people quickly adapted to living in such a cold and empty place. They became experts at hunting the mammoths that wandered across the plains, and they made almost everything they needed from the mammoths' bodies.

Hunting mammoths

Like other people at this time, the mammoth-hunters used a weapon called a spearthrower, which allowed them to throw their spears much farther than before. This made it possible to attack dangerous animals, such as mammoths, from a safe distance.

Mammoth-bone huts

There were few hills or caves on the plains, so the mammoth-hunters had nowhere to shelter from the snow and wind. Because hardly any trees grew there either, people had no wood to build huts. Instead, the mammoth-hunters made their homes from mammoth bones and skins.

This picture shows some mammoth-hunters and their huts.

Animal furs keep the hut dry and warm.

People light fires by knocking two stones together.

Mammoth tusk

Mammoth jaw bone

This man is teaching children how to throw a spear.

Spearthrower made from bone

Music and dancing

The mammoth-hunters made some of the first musical instruments that we know about. They used mammoth skulls and shoulder bones as drums, and hollowed out small bones to make flutes.

People probably danced to the music. Dancing may have been a way of bringing everyone in the tribe closer together. It may also have been part of a religious ceremony.

Mammoth-hunters playing music and dancing ★

Flute made from a hollowed-out bone

People have sewn feathers onto their clothes for the dance.

Mammoth-skull drum

This man is making a stone knife.

These women are making necklaces from shells and animal teeth.

Warm clothes

In the winter, the mammoth-hunters wore warm leather clothes made from mammoth skins sewn tightly together. They also wore leather boots and fur mittens.

Shells and beads

Sometimes, people sewed seashells or feathers onto their clothes. They also made strings of beads from shells and animal teeth, and used ivory from mammoth tusks to make bracelets. These decorated clothes and ornaments may have been worn at religious ceremonies, and tribe leaders may have had their own special decorations.

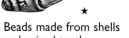

Beads made from shells and animal teeth ★

HUMANS

89

The First Artists

Around 35,000 years ago, people began to paint pictures on the walls of caves. Cave paintings have been found in many parts of the world, but the most famous ones are in France and Spain. Nobody knows why these pictures were created, but tribes may have used the painted caves for meetings and ceremonies.

Painting caves

The first paints were made by grinding soft rocks into a paste. Artists used their fingers to draw the outline of a painting. Then, they shaded in the picture by dipping a piece of animal fur in paint and pressing it onto the cave wall.

The first priests?

Sometimes, artists painted strange creatures that seem to be part human and part animal. These paintings may be portraits of early priests dressed as animals. Tribes may have held religious ceremonies in the caves where these figures were painted.

This picture shows the kind of ceremony that may have taken place in a painted cave.

This man is a priest.

Deer antler

Birds' feathers

Wolf's tail

The people are asking their gods for help with their hunting.

Painted animals

Most of the cave paintings show animals, such as bison, deer, horses and mammoths. People may have thought that the painted animals were magical and would bring them luck with their hunting.

Internet link: *For a website with a tour of a painted cave, go to* **www.usborne-quicklinks.com**

Only deep, dark caves are used for painting.

Bull

Horse

Herd of deer

Mammoth

Bison

An artist made these shapes by placing his hand on the wall and blowing paint around it.

The cave is lit by burning animal fat in stone bowls.

Skin painted with red soil

Body painting

As well as painting on cave walls, people used bright red soil to decorate dead bodies before they were buried. They may also have painted themselves with sacred symbols before taking part in religious ceremonies.

Making models

Early artists carved small statues from ivory or bone. Many of the statues show women, who may represent goddesses, and others show animals.

Ivory model of a person with a lion's head

Baking clay

Around this time, artists also discovered how to harden clay by baking it. Clay models of people and animals have been found in eastern Europe.

The first calendars?

Experts have found pieces of bone and antler with lots of tiny shapes carved on them. The shapes were carved by early people, and they seem to show the changing shape of the moon at different times of the month. Perhaps these carvings were the first calendars?

From Hunting to Farming

Around 12,000 years ago, the last ice age began to come to an end. All over the world, the weather became warmer, and the ice melted away in many areas. Huge forests began to grow where the ice had been.

After the ice age ended, some big animals, such as mammoths, died out. People had to rely on hunting deer, wild pigs and other small animals.

Most people moved around to find food, staying in a different place each season. However, some tribes of people found places where they could hunt animals, catch fish and gather plants throughout the year. This meant that these tribes could settle down and live in the same place all the time.

This picture shows a tribe of hunters living in a forest.

Taming animals

People may have started to tame horses during the last ice age. Later, hunters took baby wolves back to their camp and looked after them. The wolves began to see people as their friends, and they became tame. The wolves' babies grew up to be tame as well, and eventually these animals became working dogs. Hunters used the dogs to help them find and kill wild animals.

This ice age carving seems to show a horse wearing a harness. This suggests that early people may have tamed horses.

These people are using sticks to knock down nuts from a tree.

This girl has taken some honey from a bees' nest.

These women are gathering fruit and berries.

Wooden bowl

People use stone axes to chop up wood.

Canoe made from a tree trunk

Fishing net made from vines

These men are hunting birds with bows and arrows.

Tents made from branches and animal skins

Bowstring made of animal gut

This wild pig was caught in a pit in the forest.

Tame hunting dogs

Arrow with a stone point

Feathers make the arrows travel straight through the air.

Keeping herds

Some people began to tame lots of different animals, and eventually tribes started keeping herds of sheep, goats and cattle. This meant that people always had meat to eat and milk to drink, as well as fur and skins to make clothes.

Growing crops

Around 10,000 years ago, some tribes in the Middle East began to plant seeds and grow crops, such as wheat and barley. Once they had discovered farming, people could grow their own food, as well as going hunting and fishing.

Starting to settle

Groups of early farmers settled near the fields where their crops grew. They built huts for themselves and shelters for their animals. This was the beginning of village life.

HUMANS

93

Word List

This list explains some of the words that are used in the book.

amphibian An animal that can live on land, but lays its eggs in water. Frogs are amphibians.

arthropod A creature with jointed legs and a hard, outer skeleton. Spiders and insects are arthropods.

carnivore An animal that only eats meat.

cells The tiny "building blocks" from which all living things are made.

colony A group made up of large numbers of one kind of plant or animal. All the members of a colony live or grow together.

continent A large area of land on the surface of the Earth. Africa and North America are two of the Earth's continents.

ectothermic A word used to describe cold-blooded creatures that cannot produce their own body heat.

endothermic A word used to describe warm-blooded animals that can produce their own body heat.

evolve To change or develop gradually.

extinct A word used to describe a creature or plant that has died out. Dinosaurs are extinct.

fossil The remains of a prehistoric creature or plant. Fossils are often made of stone.

fossilize To turn into a fossil.

gills The parts of an underwater creature that take in oxygen from the water.

hadrosaur A plant-eating dinosaur with bird-like feet and a beak shaped like a duck's bill.

herbivore An animal that only eats plants.

hominid An ape that has a large brain and walks upright. Humans are hominids.

ice age A period of time when large parts of the Earth were covered with ice.

ichthyosaur A sea reptile that was shaped like a dolphin.

mammal An animal with hair on its body that feeds its babies with milk. Dogs and humans are mammals.

mammoth A large, early elephant with long, curved tusks.

marsupial A mammal whose babies stay in a pouch on their mother's stomach until they are large enough to survive on their own. Kangaroos are marsupials.

meteorite A lump of rock that falls to Earth from space.

ornithopod A plant-eating dinosaur with bird-like feet and a beak.

oxygen A gas that all living creatures need to breathe.

particle A tiny speck.

photosynthesis The process that plants use to make food from water and sunlight.

placental A mammal whose babies grow inside their mother's belly until they are large enough to survive in the outside world. Rabbits and humans are placentals.

planet A huge ball of rock, gas or metal that spins around a star.

plesiosaur A sea reptile that had a long neck and big, paddle-shaped flippers.

predator An animal that hunts and eats other animals.

prey An animal that is hunted by another animal for food.

primate A mammal with hands and feet and a large brain. Apes and humans are primates.

proteins Chemicals that form part of all living cells.

pterosaur A prehistoric reptile that could fly.

reptile An animal with scaly skin that lays its eggs on land. Lizards and snakes are reptiles.

rodent A mammal with very strong teeth that gnaws on roots, bushes and tree trunks.

sauropod A large, plant-eating dinosaur that had a long neck and tail and walked mainly on four legs.

scavenger A creature that eats meat from dead animals that it finds.

species A group of similar plants or animals that can breed together. Lions are one species and tigers are another.

stegosaur A large, plant-eating dinosaur with a row of upright bony plates along its back.

theropod A meat-eating dinosaur.

vertebrate An animal with a backbone.

Index

The names of individual creatures or plants are shown in *italic* type.

Photo credits: ©Digital Vision, 4, 11, 16 *(bottom left)*, 30, 51, 67; FPG International, 10; Dr. Kari Lounatmaa/Science Photo Library, 16 *(top left)*; ©Novosti (London), 68; ©Bill O'Connor/Still Pictures, 15; ©Planet Earth Pictures/Peter Scoones, 23; Sinclair Stammers/Science Photo Library, 16 *(right)*, 17; ©Tony Stone Images/Bill Ivy, 65; ©Peter Weimann/Still Pictures, 59. **Cover photo credit:** ©Michael S. Yamashita/Corbis.